ISBN 978-1-330-54502-7
PIBN 10076562

1 MONTH OF
FREE
READING

at
www.ForgottenBooks.com

By purchasing this book you are eligible for one month membership to ForgottenBooks.com, giving you unlimited access to our entire collection of over 700,000 titles via our web site and mobile apps.

To claim your free month visit:

www.forgottenbooks.com/free76562

Similar Books Are Available from
www.forgottenbooks.com

NICHOLAS OF THE FLUE.

THE

AVIOUR OF THE SWISS REPUBLIC.

—

A DRAMATIC POEM,

IN FIVE ACTS.

BY

JOHN CHRISTIAN SCHAAD.

WASHINGTON, D. C.:
McGILL & WITHEROW, PRINTERS AND STEREOTYPERS.
1866.

TO

PROFESSOR HENRY W. LONGFELLOW,

This Volume

IS RESPECTFULLY INSCRIBED.

PREFACE.

The united efforts of the Swiss, and their success in repelling so formidable an invader of their country as Charles the Bold, have furnished subjects to numerous poetic effusions in English as well as in other languages. Who has not read Byron's beautiful tribute to the Swiss in Childe Harold's pilgrimage?

"Morat! the proud, the patriot field! where man
    May gaze on ghastly trophies of the slain,
    Nor blush for those who conquer'd on that plain:
    Here Burgundy bequeath'd his tombless host.
        *   *   *   *   *

    Morat and Marathon, twin names shall stand!
    They were true glory's stainless victories,
    Won by the unambitious heart and hand
    Of a proud, brotherly, and civic band,
    All unbought champions in no princely cause."

The most beautiful episode in the history of Switzerland has, however, to the author's knowledge, never been brought before the public, in a dramatic form. The greatest victory which the Swiss ever obtained, *the victory over themselves*, through the efforts of a pious, warm-hearted patriot, seems, thus far, not to have attracted the attention it deserves from poets.

The author, a native of Switzerland, having had the opportunity, from his childhood, to devote considerable time to the study of his country's history, has chosen the incident, alluded to above, as a subject for a dramatic poem, with the purpose of showing to the citizens of Switzerland's great Sister Republic, on this side of the Atlantic, how, in times of internal dissensions amongst the constituents of the Swiss Confederacy, matters were brought to a peaceful issue to the satisfaction of all contending parties, preventing, thus, a civil war which would have brought ruin and desolation upon the country.

The author also takes this opportunity to give expression to his feelings of gratitude to the Government of Switzerland for the exceedingly interesting and valuable documents, furnished to him from the archives of different Cantons, and sent through the Swiss Consulate General in Washington, to assist him in bringing a glorious episode of the history of "Old Free Switzerland," in a new form, before the American public.

WASHINGTON, D. C., *December* 1, 1865.

Dramatis Personæ.

NICHOLAS OF THE FLUE, a hermit.

HENRY IM GRUND, the pastor of Stanz, in the Canton of Unterwalden.

ARNOLD, his brother, a peasant in Unterwalden.

MARY, }
LILY, } Arnold's daughters.

ALOYS, his adopted son.

ADRIAN VON BUBENBERG, ex-Lord Provost of Berne.

JULIA, his daughter.

EDWARD, his son.

RUDOLPH, his page.

NICHOLAS VON SCHARNACHTHAL, Lord Provost of Berne.

WILLIAM VON DIESSBACH, }
PETERMANN VON WABERN, } ex-Lords Provost.

RUDOLPH VON ERLACH, }
PETERMANN VON STEIN, } Senators of Berne.

HANNS WALDMANN, of Zürich, commander-in-chief of the Swiss forces.

JOHN VON HALLWYL, a nobleman of Berne.

CASPAR VON HERTENSTEIN, of Lucerne.

LOUIS, Count of Gruyères.

HANNS IMHOF, }
HANNS ZUMBRUNNEN, } of Uri.

RAETZI, Landammann, }
DIETRICH INDERHALDEN, } of Schwytz.

PAUL ENNENTACHER,
HENRY ZELGER, } of Unterwalden.

HANNS LANDENBERG, of Zürich.

HANNS TSCHUDI, of Glaris.

HANNS ITEN, of Zug.

ULRIC VON HOHENSAX, of Argovy.

PETER ROT, of Basil.

JACOB BUGNIET, of Friburgh.

HANNS VON STAAL,
HEMMANN HAGEN, } of Soleure.

FOSTER, of Bienne.

WILLIAM HERTER, of Strasburgh.

LOUIS, Count of Oettingen.

OSWALD, Count of Thierstein.

RENÉ OF ANJOU, Duke of Lorraine.

CHARLES THE BOLD, Duke of Burgundy.

ANTHONY, his half-brother.

THOMAS, Duke of Somerset,
WILLIAM, Prince of Orange,
OLIVIER DE LA MARCHE,
CREVECOEUR,
RUBEMPRÉ,
COUNT CAMPOBASSO,
} Officers of Charles.

ASTRADAMUS, an astrologer

A page.

Senators of Berne; bannerets of the eight Cantons; two sergeants-at-arms; a chancellor and two secretaries of the Senate of Berne; three priests of the Minster of St. Vincent; women, children, and old men of Berne; soldiers of the Swiss Confederacy and their allies; peasants and herdsmen of Unterwalden.

TIME:

FROM A. D. 1476 TO 1482.

ACT I.

The orchestra plays the air of the Switzer's Farewell. Whilst the last sounds are lingering, the curtain slowly rises and presents to the eye a landscape scene in the Canton of Unterwalden, not far from the frontiers of the territory of Berne. In the foreground is a substantial rustic dwelling house, with open windows. The inscription, "*Deo soli gloria*," is painted in large letters above the door. A flower garden is behind the house, from which gradually rises a hill, covered with pine trees. In the distance are seen a few peaks of the Bernese Alps, glowing in the light of the rising sun.

ALOYS is standing on the summit of the hill, and plays the last strains of the Switzer's Farewell on the Alpine horn. He then descends. When he arrives before the house, the church bell in the distance rings the Angelus. ALOYS kneels down with head uncovered. The orchestra plays a slow and plaintive symphony.

Mary. (*sings within the house.*)
>Ave Maria!
>Queen of my soul!
>Mother of mercy,
>Mother of God.
>Full of His graces,

Here in the morning,
Call we on thee.
Pray for us sinners,
Now and when dying!
Ave Maria:
Queen of my soul!

(ALOYS *arises;* MARY *appears at the door.*)

Aloys. Exalted be the name of Jesus Christ.
Mary. Forever more, amen![1]

(*Both remain silent and appear lost in contemplation of the scene in the distance.*)

Aloys.   How beautiful!
The morning sun is greeting here the land,
As one to which he loves to show himself
At first.   The Finsteraarhorn's pointed peak,
The Youngfrau, lofty, grand, majestic, like
A virgin queen—reflect his earliest beams
On adamantine crystal brows, as if
The land of freedom were most dear to him.

Mary. Yes, beautiful is this, our native land,
And worthy to be loved by all that are
Allowed to dwell within its happy bounds;
It seems to be JEHOVAH's favoured child.

Aloys. With bounteous hand HE hath bestowed
                    on us
The choicest blessings—Liberty, and strength
Of arm to wield the mighty sword in her

Defence.   What glorious lore is taught to all
The world by Switzerland!   What heroes' names
Presents her history to be embalmed
Forever in the mem'ry of her child!
The names of Tell, of Melchthal, Winkelried,
Of d'Erlach, Bubenberg, and Scharnachthal.

Mary. Alas! I fear we may become too proud,
And thus upon us bring the wrath of Him
Who giveth grace to humble worth.   I fear
We may forget that all the blessings we
Enjoy, the victories our fathers' arms,
And we ourselves, have won on battle-fields,
Were naught but GOD ALMIGHTY's gracious boon
To humble praying granted in distress.

Aloys. 'Tis true; this fear I often feel myself,
Not here—for these, our peaceful valleys, where
Simplicity and frugal life have dwelt
For ages, where the peasant's honest heart
And sound, judicious sense ignores the great
Temptations, crimes, corruption, found in proud
And haughty cities, joined to Uri, Schwytz
And Unterwalden's league.

Mary.   Methinks, my friend
Is most severe on allies who have brought
Much honor to our land.   Dost thou forget
That d'Erlach, Bubenberg, and Scharnachthal
Are lords of noble Berne?   Have they not fought
At Unterwalden's side on Granson's day?

Aloys. Excuse my speech!   At Unterwalden's side
They did not fight, but she at their's, to help
That lordly Berne against the host, arrayed
By Charles the Bold to crush the haughty town.

  Mary. Be not unjust!   That Berne is proud, I
            grant,
But haughty—no!   Remember all her past:
Alone she stood against the Habsburgh's host,
Against the nobles all at Donnerbuehl[2]
And Laupen's bloody field,[3] where d'Erlachs twice
Defeated Freedom's foes.

  Aloys.   Was Berne, the proud,
On Sempach's sacred ground?   Hath she a name
Like—Winkelried?

  Mary.   Beware!   Dost thou pronounce
This hallowed name with rev'rence due?   Dost thou
Recall to mind to whom our fathers prayed
On that immortal day, before they rushed
Upon the Austrian host?

  Aloys.   I do, but still
I love to hear thy lips repeat the words
By pray'r addressed to Him, on whom we look,
With holy awe and gratitude profound,
As on our nation's Saviour, Jesus Christ.

  Mary. Oh, may the words until the end of time
Be graved in every Switzer's heart, and thus
Proclaim to nations all, that Freedom's home
Is Christian land, and ever must be so!

(ARNOLD IM GRUND *appears, unobserved by* MARY *and* ALOYS.
He listens with profound attention.)

Mary. (*With eyes uplifted, and with great emotion.*)
    Oh, Bounteous Christ in Heaven !
    By Thy most awful death,
    We, miserable sinners, ⌐
    In peril and distress,
    Beseech Thee in our anguish
    To stand at our side !
    Assist us in preserving
    A shield for our land!
    Protection to our people
    Oh, Christ, in mercy grant. (*Weeps.*)
Arnold. (*Coming forward.*) My child, thou speakest
    well. The Switzer's firm
Belief shall ever be that his extolled
Redeemer heard the humble band before
Whom haughty Austria fell. The standard high,
The Switzer's banner bears the Christian sign—
The CROSS. And this is Christian soil. No man
That feels ashamed to wear that honored sign
Here on his breast and on his arm, is fit
To be a citizen in Switzerland.

    Lily. (*Dressed in white with a blue ribbon around her
    waist, comes out of the house.*)
Good morrow, father! darling Mary, come—

  2

Give me my morning kiss! What now, my own
Beloved sister weeps?

Mary. (*Pressing Lily to her heart.*) Be silent, child!
I weep the tears of joy to be, alike
Thyself a Switzer's daughter, freed by Christ's
Most glorious sign.

Aloys. (*With enthusiasm.*) What might, in earth or
        hell,
Will stand against the CROSS!

Lily.   Oh, Mary dear,
Shall I not tell what lovely dream I had,
Before I did awake this morning?

Mary.   Tell,
Sweet child, thy dream!

Lily   Methought I saw above
The snowy mountain yonder—what's its name?

Aloys. The Youngfrau, child.

Lily.   The Holy Virgin stand,
With arms outspread, as if to bless the vales
Beneath. Oh, beautiful she looked amidst
A host of angels lovely!

Mary. (*Embracing Lily.*) Child, dear child,
To such like thee, the blessed Heavenly Queen
Does love to show herself in slumbers sweet.

Lily. And then I saw above her head, with stars
Adorned as with a crown—a brilliant CROSS,
As white as snow, in sunbeams' shine, and on

SCENE II.

The forest of Ranft in Unterwalden. The hermitage of NICHOLAS OF THE FLUE is seen near a small chapel in the background. The wild torrent of the Melch forms a cascade, and then flows through a ravine, over which is erected a narrow bridge. NICHOLAS OF THE FLUE and HENRY IM GRUND, the pastor of Stanz, are sitting on the trunk of a fallen tree.

Henry. 'Tis as I said, no hope for peace.

Nicholas.   . It grieves
My heart to hear the news my father brings.
I hoped that Charles, the noble Duke, for once
Would learn, by his defeat, on Granson's field,
That God resists the haughty.   Pride hath brought
To fall the mightiest houses, princes, kings,
Empires and commonwealths, from earliest times.

Henry. Alas! that man will never learn the old
Eternal lesson, taught by Holy Writ
And all the Christian fathers!

Nicholas.   Charles the Bold,
Is he prepared again to come, invade,
With force sufficient, Switzerland?   I thought,
Perhaps, his losses were so great, that now
He would be glad to treat for peace.   His lands
Have suffered much by all his wars.

Henry.   They say,
He seems to be bereft of self-control;
In dark and gloomy musings lost, from time
To time, alike some furious wounded beast

That snaps at friend and foe, he will give vent
To fiercest rage and temper wild 'gainst all
That dare or are obliged to draw anear
His person.   Spurning all his friends' advice,
He still is bent on naught but stern revenge.

    Nicholas. Revenge 'gainst whom?   The hand of
       GOD?   Poor Charles!

    Henry. 'Tis said that every man of six in his
Dominions all, is called to arms; the sixth
Of every pence is levied.   Where the bells
Of churches seem in sound estate, and where,
In houses, iron kettles more than one
Are found,—they all are seized for casting guns.
The Duchess of Savoy, Iolanta, still
Assists him.   Louis, King of France, the one
Who was the secret cause of all the strife
Between the Duke and Switzerland, is now
Evasive, vague, uncertain, wily, full
Of artful words in all he says, afraid
To break with Charles.   The Emperor himself
Is trying to retard the measures which
The Swiss might take.

    Nicholas.   'Tis not on foreign help
The Swiss must count, rely.   Their strength is found
Within themselves.   What say my gracious lords
Of Berne?

    Henry. In Berne confusion seems to reign.
The Provosts Diessbach, Scharnachthal are both

For hot pursuit of war, but Bubenberg,
The noble stately lord, suspected friend
Of Charles, from council hath withdrawn, retir'd
To Spiez, his own ancestral seat.

(ALOYS *and* MARY *emerge from the forest.*)

What now !
You children here ?   I thought that you had left
The church for home.
    Mary.   I love to come, on days
Like this, in your wild solitude, to see
Our most revered, beloved, faithful friend
The far-famed brother Claus.
    Nicholas.   The likes of thee,
My child, are ever welcome here.
    Mary.   And he,
My brother Aloys?
    Nicholas.   Is welcome, too.
You both are dear to me, but where and how
Is she, thy little sister Lily ?
    Mary.   Well !
She went with father home from church.
    Aloys.   Alike
Her graceful namesake which exhales her sweet
Perfume, in gratitude on high, for her
Creation, this beloved child, with thoughts
Angelic, pure, delights us all and seems
To make us breathe the air of spheres divine.

Mary. (*Smiling.*) What music in thy words! How
    well thou couldst
Expound to man the truth of God!

Aloys.   Beware!

Mary. My worthy fathers both; we come to ask
For your advice. I think my brother here
Is now of age to choose the path of life
He ought to take

Henry.   Indeed! the boy has grown
To be a man.

Nicholas. (*Musingly.*) How flies the time! It
    seems
To me but yesterday I took him, then
A babe, to Arnold's house.

Mary.   I deem 't is wrong
That he, with talents great, with knowledge deep
Endowed, should spend his life in toil obscure
In these, our valleys, like a peasant, or
A herdsman.

Henry.   Proud, ambitious girl! For him—
What nobler calling could be wished?

Mary.   Your own!

Henry. What he, you mean, he should become a
    Priest?

Mary. Is there a calling higher in the world
Than that of him, who is a guide to man's
Immortal soul, a father mild, a judge
Of right and wrong? he comforts the distressed,

Uplifts the fallen, and diffuses life
Celestial in Holy Sacrament.

   Henry.   True!
But feels the boy, within his inmost heart,
A call to serve the LORD, renounce the world
With all its charms?

   Aloys.   Alas! my father, no.!

   Mary. I fear, thou knowest not thyself, my
       friend!
Thy soul is far too great to be absorbed
In love of things terrestrial. Love of GOD
Alone can quench thy thirst.

   Aloys.   'Tis thy mistake,
My heart does yearn for earthly love, for one
That may respond, with tenderness sincere,
To all I feel, and gladden once a home
To me.

   Nicholas. (*To Mary.*) Beware, lest thou mislead
       the boy!
It is an awful thing to be a priest
Of GOD! The Bride of Christ rejects the heart
That fluctuates between the world and her.

   Henry. Alas! how few will think of this, before
They take upon themselves the sacred vows!
How deep the fall of some hath been! Disgrace
And shame they brought upon the Church, and
       vice
Most vile into her sanctuary's halls;

The Holy See itself hath been defiled
By men unfit for their vocation high.
What unclean vessels for the source of life!

  Nicholas. Saint Peter fell! and yet he had been
   called
The Rock on which the Church shall ever stand.
The source of Life may flow through veins of lead
Or gold; its healing waters still remain
The same. Whatever men may do to bring
Disgrace upon their sacred calling,—she,
The Church of Christ forevermore will stand
Aloft, immaculate and pure, in all
Her bridal beauty.

  Henry.   True, Saint Peter fell!
But he redeemed his fall by martyr's death.
The Church had then her foes without, but now
They are within herself. Corruption stains
Her priests and prelates. Nay! the Pope hath been
Accused of crimes atrocious. Sacred vows
Of nuns and monks to live a chaste, and pure,
And virtuous life, are spurned and ridiculed.
I, trembling, see a mighty storm approach,
That will, with rage and fury, shake the Church
To her foundation.

  Nicholas.   Let it come! The storm
But purifies the air. The Church will stand
As firm as yonder snowy peaks, the Alps.
The SON OF GOD hath promised to abide

With her until this earth shall be no more.
JEHOVAH reigns!   Who dares to doubt His word?

(*Thunder is heard in the distance.* HENRY, ALOYS, *and* MARY *look with amazement at the hermit, who stands erect, with eyes uplifted to heaven.*)

Mary. (*Whispering to Aloys.*)   Behold! What fiery
 glow is on his face!
As one transfigured, there he stands!
Aloys.   And God
Almighty thunders Amen to his words.

(*All remain silent for awhile.*)

Henry. My children, dark becomes the sky.   We
 are
Too late to reach our homes, before the storm
Will burst upon the valley.   Here we may
A shelter take in yonder chapel.   See!
The rain begins to fall, and lightning rends
The clouds.
Mary. 'Tis meet to kneel in humble pray'r,
When God, in mighty voice, reminds us all
Of His omnipotence and majesty.

            [*Exeunt.*]

3

SCENE III.

A wild forest. A path winds itself from the summit of a hill, in the background, to its base. The rain is violently swept by the wind through the trees. Thunder and lightning. EDWARD VON BUBENBERG, in a hunting dress, and with a cross-bow strapped over his shoulder, appears on the top of the hill, and slowly descends the path. He is lame, and leans on an Alpine staff. Arriving at the foot of the hill, he sinks exhausted on the ground.

Edward. I can no more. Here must I die. Oh
  GOD!
Away from home, from father, sister, friends!
Oh, awful fate! deserved by reckless wish
For roving, hunting, 'midst the forest wild!
Two days have gone since, lost within the woods,
I've neither tasted food, nor other drink
But water. GOD! Is there no help? To die—
To be a prey to ravenous beast! Oh GOD!
My GOD! Forgive my sins! Remember not
The failings of my youth! If Thou would'st still
Vouchsafe, in mercy, help to send, I vow
To make a pilgrimage to Holy Land.
It is too late! My sight grows dim. The pangs
Of death approach. Oh! holy Virgin, pray
For me!

Of aspirations lofty, eagle-like,
And as a lion bold and brave, with mind
Imperial, proud, I grant, but just. He was
His country's idol, chivalrous in all
He did; a hero whom the ancients would
Have ranked amongst the gods. I loved that Charles;
I love him still.

  Julia.   Your country's foe?

  Adrian.   Alas!

He was not always that; but listen, child!
We often would review the past, converse
On Greek and Roman heroes great. The names
Of Alexander, Hannibal, inspired
With high, enthusiastic ardor both
Of us. But, more than all, the name of one
Appeared most dear to Charles.

  Julia.   Whose name?

  Adrian.   ' The name

Of Julius Cæsar. Ah! in him he seemed
To live, to breathe. Th' illustrious hero's works
He daily read. What others wrote of him,
In prose or verse, he quoted. Once I heard
My friend describe the scene of Cæsar's death.
With count'nance pale, with eyes in tears, he gazed
On me. In broken voice I heard him say:
" And Brutus, thou!" That look, that thrilling tone
Hath haunted ever since my mind.

(RUDOLPH, *the page, enters and presents several letters on a salver* to
ADRIAN.)

Rudolph.   My lord,
The messenger from Berne hath come and brought
The missives here

Adrian. 'Tis well; thou can'st withdraw; but tell:
That madcap boy of mine—hath he returned?

Rudolph. Lord Edward? No, not yet.

Julia.   In truth, I feel
Alarmed. 'Twas fifteen days ago he left
The castle.

Adrian. Never fear! Ill weed will grow,
Not perish.

Julia. Father! Edward is not bad,
Not vicious. Wild and reckless he may be,
But still he has a heart as tender, warm,
As ever beat. His fault is spirit high,
Exuberance of strength, the Switzer's gift.
He wants a field to act, a chance to win
A name. This peaceful life at home is not
The one for him.

Adrian.   He wants to go abroad,
To see the world, until, afar from home,
He will, with longing soul, regret the step.
Which made him leave his Fatherland. Alas!
The Switzer learns to feel the magic spell,
His country throws around his heart, but when
Abroad!

(*Opening one of the letters.*)

But what is this?   What hast thou done?
Mischievous girl?   Indeed, surprise and sport
And honor too, is here for thee.   A German prince
Of old descent, immensely rich, requests,
In terms most formal, courteous, me to give
His son—thy hand.

    Julia. (*In a tone of vexation.*)   I know of whom
        you speak,
I met that son of him who writes, in Berne.
I sometimes danced with him at balls.   He is
A youth effeminate, and oily-tongued,
And dressed in costly silks and velvets; wears
Around his neck such chains of gold, enough
To make him sweat beneath their weight, with hair
In curls perfumed, affected in his speech.
I noticed not the flattering things he said
To me, and thus I did not deem it worth
To say a word to you.

    Adrian.   Why, girl, dost thou,
In terms of such contempt, allude to one
That pays to thee the highest compliment
A man can pay to woman?   Answer me;
Dost thou refuse the honor offered here?

    Julia. I do, and more, I feel insulted, vexed,
That such a silly fool should dare, presume
To think that I might be entranced by charms
Like his.

Adrian. His rank and wealth may——

Julia.   What of rank?

No man who thinks an honor to bestow
On me shall ever have my hand.

Adrian.   But child!

Hast thou considered well?——

Julia.   I do not love

The man.   I cannot love him, never will.
I do despise him now.

Adrian.   What nonsense, girl!

Who thinks of love, in days like these, when rank
And wealth are first to be considered?   Love!
Is there such thing as love?   I thought that thou
Didst not believe in fancy whims as love.

Julia. My father wrongs himself in speech so
          strange.

Would he have dared, in words like these, to woo
My sainted mother?   Love; ah, sacred flame!
Creation's essence, yea! thou dost exist.
The loveliest, sweetest fragrance from the heart
Proceeds from thee.   Thou art the highest boon
On earth bestowed on man, the tie that links
To immortality his soul.

Adrian.   What bard

Or minstrel hath been here to sing such strains
To thee?   Perhaps at last thy heart is touched.
That handsome Duke René, whose cause, in Berne,

The women all will plead, hath cast an eye
On thee.

 Julia. No mortal's image yet is here
Enshrined within my heart. I do not like
To hear you speak with levity of love—
And marriage. GOD hath sanctioned both. His
  Church,
In Holy Sacrament, unites in bonds
Most beautiful, indissoluble, man
And woman, noblest creatures still of Him
Who first the world created; strength and grace
United here by sacred rites, enhance
The realms of happiness on earth, prepare
The soul for higher bliss in Heav'n above.

 Adrian. (*Aside; musingly.*) Her sainted mother!
   How like her she looks
Her own, her very words she but repeats.
(*To Julia.*) Forgive, my child, for having thus dis-
  turbed
Thy soul serene with mere ambitions whims
To see, my child—a princess!

 Julia.   Princess, I!
My father can forget, whose blood doth flow
Within my veins, forget who is himself?
The prince is but the vassal of a king;
On their estates, the lords of Berne themselves
Are kings!

 Adrian. Oh, glorious girl! Come here into

My arms!   Thou art, indeed, of Bubenbergs'
The worthy issue.

   Julia.   Father, now I know
You are yourself again.   Your heart is right,
Would disapprove of sacrilegious bonds.
The woman who, for sordid motives, will
Degrade herself, pronounce a lie before
The altar, brings the curse of GOD upon
Her house.   I feel no wish for change of life,
No wish to leave my native land.   I love
My country,—love it!   Like the morning star
Of liberty, it shines to nations all.
With you, in this our home, I'm happy still.
The time may come, when I shall meet the soul
To which my own is tuned in harmony.
Do promise me to let the choice be mine,
To let me link my fate to one I love!

   Adrian. I do, my child!

   Rudolph (*Enters.*)   My lord, a peasant youth
Is here from Unterwalden, asking leave
To see your lordship.

   Adrian.   Well! his name?

   Rudolph.   Im Grund.

   Adrian. Im Grund!   I know that name.   Admit
      the youth!

(ALOYS, *dressed in peasant's costume, enters and bows with stateliness to* JULIA, *and then to her father.*)

Aloys. Your lordship's most obedient.

Julia. (*Aside with surprise.*) What? Is this
A peasant? Look what noble mien! what hands
And feet so small! what lordly eagle eye!

Adrian. Be welcome, friend! Are you, perhaps,
    akin
To one I often saw in Berne, on days
When delegates, from all the Cantons, met
In council hall—Arnold Im Grund?

Aloys.   I am
My lord, his son adopted.

Adrian.   Here, your hand,
My friend! A worthier man than he breathes not
In Unterwalden. Page, a cup of wine—
A chair!

(RUDOLPH *draws an arm-chair to the centre of the hall, then leaves for a moment, and reappears with a salver, on which he bears a large silver cup, which he presents to* ALOYS.)

Aloys. Your health, my lady! your's, my lord!
                        (*Drinks.*)

Julia. (*Aside.*)   What ease,
What grace, what dignity in all he does!

Aloys. (*Drawing a letter from his pocket.*)
    My lord, I bring a message here for you;

A letter written by your Lordship's son,
Who ill is lying in my father's house.

 Adrian. My son! (*Seizing the letter and opening it
  hurriedly.*)

 Julia.   My brother ill?

 Adrian. (*Reading.*) " These lines will be
Presented by the saviour of my life."

 Julia. My brother's saviour, you? Oh speak!
  What ill
Befell him?

 Adrian. (*Reading*) " Hunting in the mountains
  wild
I lost my way, when I had crossed the pass
Of Brünig, in a forest dense. Without
A morsel there to eat, the second day,
Exhausted I had sunk and swooned away,
And given up myself as lost "

 Julia.   Poor boy!

 Adrian. " The Blessed Virgin must have heard my
  words—
My last, in praying, uttered. Angels like
This youth you see, his lovely sister, with
A reverend father, found me, took me up,
And led me to their home. For sev'ral days
I lay in fever most severe; but now
I'm out of danger; weak, 'tis true, but care
Most tender here is taken of your son."

Julia. (*Seizing with emotion the hand of Aloys.*)
You saved my brother's life! No words can tell—
Express my gratitude to you.

    Adrian.   Nor mine.
My friend, we are your debtors all. My son
Is now your father's guest; you must be mine,
At least until my boy returns.

    Aloys.   You are
Too kind, my lord. My message done, I must
Return. We are in May. My father's herd
Shall leave, next week, the valley for the Alps.
I must be there.

    Julia. (*Aside.*) A herdsman merely—he?

    Rudolph. (*Enters.*) My Lord von Hallwyl.

    Adrian.   John, my dearest friend,
What lucky star brings thee?

    Von Hallwyl.   No lucky star
This time.

(*Perceiving* ALOYS, *he goes towards him and grasps warmly his hand.*)

             You here? What gladdening surprise!

    Adrian. You know my friend?

    Von Hallwyl.   What, know him?
         'tis the brave,
The noble herdsman who, midst heroes all,
On Granson's battle-field, the bravest, dared—
When victory was won, and Scharnachthal,
My Lord Provost of Berne, the eldest knight,

On Waldmann and myself bestowed the boon
Of knighthood, dared—when he was called **to kneel,**
And to receive the lordly title too,
Dared to decline the honor.

   Julia.   Noble men
Of nature titles never need.

   Aloys.   My Lords:
Forgive! I am an humble herdsman **poor,**
An orphan child, adopted by Im' Grund,
A worthy peasant, who from Brother Claus
A hermit——

   Adrian. Brother Claus, I know him **well;**
He is the wisest man in Switzerland,
The holiest too.

   Aloys.   —Received me when a babe.
My parents are unknown to me.   My **name**
In secret keeps the Brother Claus alone.
I know it not, and thus I thought I had
No right to take the honor offer'd me.

   Adrian. No matter who you are, you saved **my son.**
He is the last of Bubenbergs.

   Von Hallwyl. (*To Adrian.*) My friend,
I am in haste.   I wish to have a word,
On state affairs, with you alone

   Adrian. (*To Aloys.*)   At all
Events you shall not leave to-day.   Remain
With Julia here, my daughter, till **the bell**
Will call to dinner!

(*Exeunt* ADRIAN *and* VON HALLWYL.)

Julia. (*After a few moments of silence.*)   Thus **the**
   herdsman's life
Is all to you ?   No higher aim you have ?
   Aloys. It is a peaceful, happy, modest life
That giveth time to deep and solemn thought,
To meditations on the mysteries
The world presents.   The greatest men of old
Were herdsmen.   Kings were not ashamed to **guard**
Their flocks in Greece and Rome.   To herdsmen first
The King of kings vouchsafed to show himself
At Bethlehem.
   Julia. (*Aside.*)   What strange bewitching **spell**
In all his words!

(*Enter again* ADRIAN *and* VON HALLWYL.)

Adrian. (*Whispering.*)   It cannot be, **my friend!**

ALOYS *has risen from his seat, and is looking at the volume on the
stand before the arm chair.*

Von Hallwyl. Your Fatherland in peril will **you**
   leave—
Forsake?
   Adrian. My Fatherland hath spurned my **own**
Advice in proper time.   This war then might
Have been avoided.
   Von Hallwyl.   Bubenberg, you know,
In council on this point, we did agree.
Like you, I was opposed to French **intrigue**
   4*

And bribery.   I am no friend of him,
That sneaking Louis, king of France.

   Adrian.   **It is**
Enough to move the stones, to see the bold
And manly, honest, gen'rous, candid heart
Entangled by the snares of such a cur,
A hypocrite——

   Julia.   My father!

   Adrian.   Child, I know
I will forget myself, when kings descend
To play the fox.   And Brutus, thou!

   Von Hallwyl. (*Pointing to the portraits on the wall.*)
                          Behold!
Your fathers look upon you here.   They all
Have stood to Berne in danger's hour.   Your friend,
The Duke, hath not alone offended Berne;
He tramples on the rights of man, on all
That's sacred to humanity.

   Aloys. (*Reading aloud.*)   " All men,
By nature, freedom love and hate to be
In servitude."   Ah, Cæsar! hads't thou thought
Of this at Rome, no Brutus might have been.

   Adrian. (*With astonishment.*)
A herdsman reading, quoting Cæsar!   Who
Hath mentioned names like these to you?

   Aloys. My lord, be not surprised!   I learned the
      tongue

Of ancient Rome, in winter evenings long,
From worthy Father Henry, Priest of Stanz.

 Von Hallwyl. The country is in danger, friends,
  again.
The Duke of Burgundy, with stronger force,
Than once before, prepares to come. They say
He does advance with eighty thousand men,
Besiege the town of Morat. Cavalry,
The best of England, headed by the Duke
Of Somerset, he hath engaged. With guns
Of siege five hundred——

 Julia.   GOD save my country !

 Adrian. And Brutus, thou !

 Von Hallwyl.   The Duke in rage hath sworn
He will exterminate the commonwealth
Of Berne, and force again beneath his sway
The world. As Cæsar he will rule. Shall Berne
Submit ?

 Adrian. (*Laboring under violent struggle with himself,*
  takes the sword from the wall, unsheathes it, and
  comes to the centre of the scene.)
   No ! Cæsar's arm shall never rule
In Berne ! A commonwealth of nobles proud,
And burghers, artisans, united all
By one great feeling—love of native soil—
She shall remain, as long as this my arm
Can sway the sword——

Von Hallwyl.   Oh, noble Bubenberg!

Adrian.   To future ages shall the name of Berne,
A model State, by wisdom, justice ruled,[1]
The home of freedom be bequeathed to all
Our children.   Each of them shall ever, proud
With head uplifted, royal, dare to say:
I too, was born in Berne!   The Lords of Berne
Will have no master but the King of kings.

(ADRIAN *and* VON HALLWYL *join their hands.* ALOYS *comes quietly
between them, and places his hand on theirs.*)

Aloys.   And Unterwalden stands to Berne! myself
I'll lead the van.   Nor Lords nor peasants now,
In danger one, as brothers, Switzers all
Unite against the foe to stand—or fall !

SCENE II.

Before ARNOLD IM GRUND's house in Untorwalden.   MARY is at
her knitting work ; EDWARD VON BUBENBERG sitting on a rustic
arm chair ; LILY at his side.

Lily.   My Lord, I like to hear you talk of all
Your city's wonders.

Mary.   Berne, indeed, must be
A splendid place.

Edward.   'Midst Uechtland's cities, Berne
Is like a solid wall, a bulwark strong
For lands, where freedom's day was dawning first.

Lily. Are not the people there most proud?
Edward. They are.
Lily. The Blessed Virgin was not proud.
Edward. My child:
The Lord of Berne uplifts his head 'midst men—
His equals—bows, like you, in humble faith
Before his GOD.
Mary. And justice, equity,
Have ever dwelt in Berne. Of Switzerland
The oldest noble families are there.
Edward. There is a house in which the Habsburghs
     served
As pages once. If ever you should come
To Berne, how happy I shall be to show
Her beauties all to you!
Mary. To me, my Lord,
A peasant girl?
Edward. My guardian angel, who
Has saved my life.
Mary. My Lord, you overrate
The little I have done. The one to whom
You prayed, the Blessed Virgin, sent you help.
Edward. Sent you.
Arnold. (*With hat and riding whip in his hands, ap-*
    pears.)
Oh, Lily, darling, wilt thou come
With me to visit Brother Claus? I'll seat
Thee on my horse before me.

Lily. (*Clapping her hands with joy.*) Brother Claus,
The holy man!   How happy I shall be!

(*Exeunt* ARNOLD *and* LILY.)

Edward. What pleasant, cheerful life you lead in
    this
So peaceful valley!   How I feel regret
To leave it, leave my kindest friends, and—you!
    Mary. My Lord will soon forget us in the crowd
Of Berne's bewitching beauties.
    Edward.   You, I should
Forget?   No nevermore! if I should live
A thousand years.
    Mary.   The heart of man will oft
Deceive its owner.
    Edward.   Never me!   Before
I leave, I feel compelled to say a word
To you.
    Mary. My Lord!
    Edward.   I love you, Mary, love
With all my heart——
    Mary. (*Bursting into tears.*)   My Lord, this is too
    much!
Remember who you are, and who am I!
    Edward. Have I offended you?   Forgive!   With
    heart
Sincere, most earnest, do I love.   You are
A Switzer's daughter, I—a Switzer's son.

Mary. A nobleman, a Lord of Berne!

Edward.   And you

A noble woman, lov'liest of your sex!

What change you have effected in my mind!

Your presence acts alike a soothing breeze

On me.   My reckless, stormy nature yields

At once to influence so sweet, so pure,

So holy.

Mary. Fancy's work all this may be,

My Lord.   I am an humble peasant girl,

Not used to speech so flatt'ring.

Edward.   Mary, how,

On themes like these, can you believe I use

But words of sacred truth?   When shades of death

Were threat'ning me, I made a vow to go

To see the Holy Grave——

(Bells begin to ring in the distance.   The sounds of horns are heard
from different directions.)

Mary.   Oh, Heavens! hark!

What's this?   Alarum bells, the horns of war!

(Enter again ARNOLD *and* LILY.)

My father, what, you here so soon?

Arnold.   We met

The Brother Claus not far from here.   He comes

Himself to us, and brings some serious news.

(Alarum bells in the neighborhood.   Enter ALOYS *and several young peasants and herdsmen.)*

Lily   (Rushing into the arms of Aloys.)
Oh, brother mine, what now?   You look so strange.
    Aloys. To arms, whoever bears the Switzer's name!
The horn of war is blown throughout the land.
    Arnold. What now, when spring hath just begun,
        and herds
Should go to Alps?
    Aloys.   No herds may soon be left
To guard in Unterwalden here, if Berne,
Her bulwark, falls.
    Edward.   Is Berne besieged?
    Aloys.   Not yet,
But Morat.
    Edward. What, so near?   A town but five
Short leagues from Berne.
    Aloys.   Your noble father there
Hath gone to keep, defend the place.
    Edward.   Against
His friend, the Duke?
    Aloys.   No friendship could retain
My Lord von Bubenberg from serving now
His country, when in danger.
    Edward.   Oh, and I
Am here!
    Aloys. To arms, ye men! I've pledged to Berne
The youth of Unterwalden.

Arnold. Youth is haste.
The season now is not the same as when
In March, the snow was on the Alps.

(*Enters* NICHOLAS OF THE FLUE; *all the men uncover their heads.*)

Nicholas. My friends:
The council of the Canton hath resolved
To send to Berne the banner of the land.
 All the young men. To arms! Hurrah! hurrah!
  hurrah!

(*Exeunt all but* NICHOLAS, ARNOLD, MARY, *and* LILY. *The ringing
of the bells continues. The echos of voices in different direc-
tion are heard singing:*

To arms!
To arms! to arms! hurrah!

(*Variations on the Alpine horn on the call to arms.*)

Mary. Come; Lily! thou
And I, we can but pray to GOD that He
In mercy may protect our land.

(*Exeunt.*)

Arnold. I fear,
This love of war which here our youth betray,
Will soon become a curse to Switzerland.
No more content to humble toil to give
Their strength, they rush to arms, to battle-fields,
And find their joy in shedding blood, remind
Us of the beasts, that once have tasted gore,

5

Will quench their thirst in naught besides.   I feel
Alarmed for future days.   This king of France,
That first hath offer'd gold for Switzers' arms,
Will soon corrupt our youth, and make them spurn
The toil for daily bread.

 Nicholas.   My friend is right.
I fear myself this will become a curse,
Disgrace to all the Swiss, and bring the wrath
Of GOD upon the nation.   Man was doomed
To labor, till the soil, and not to slay
His brother.   War and bloodshed take their source
From sin.

 Arnold. Methinks I heard my Brother say
That GOD is peace.

 Nicholas. And peace He is and love,
To him that leads a sinless life, but GOD
Is justice, too!   A stern avenger on
The haughty one who will defy His law,
And trample on the rights of man.

 Arnold.   In days
Of yore the Switzers went to war to stand
Against oppressors vile, defend their rights
Alone.   What now, when rulers will allow
To sell the blood of man, accept from kings
And princes—bribes as hath heen done?

 Nicholas.   For sins,
Like these, their offspring once will have to pay,
To suffer.   When the love of sordid gain,

The thirst of gold shall once possess the Swiss
To lend their arms to foreign kings, to crush—
Oppress their people, soon or late, the curse
Of GOD will fall upon the Switzers.   War
Will come—invade the land, and those on whom
The mercenaries helped to place the yoke,
Themselves will take revenge, from power hurl
The ones who bear the names of those that first
This traffic sanctioned.   Dark will be the cloud
On Switzerland, BUT SINS OF NATIONS MUST
BE DROWNED IN BLOOD !

 Arnold. (*Aside.*) What strange, prophetic words !
How sad and yet sublime he looks ! (*Aloud.*)   Is now
This awful doom to come on us ?   This war
With Charles——

   (*Enter* MARY *and* LILY, *unobserved by the speakers.*)

 Nicholas.   Is not the one of which I speak.
In war like this, the Swiss are for the right,
And GOD will help them still.
 Arnold.   Then all must take
The sword in Unterwalden.
 Mary. (*Throwing her arms around her father's neck.*)
     Father, no !
You are too old, too weak.   You cannot go.
Your wound is not yet healed.
 Arnold.   My child, I bled

On Granson's field, two months ago; I'm strong
Again.   My country calls.
   Mary.   But if you sink
In death, who then shall be my father?
   Arnold. (Pointing upward.)   GOD
In Heaven.
   Lily. (With hands crossed.)   GOD in Heaven, hear
     thy child!
Preserve, protect my father!

   (The blasts of a powerful horn are heard.)

   Arnold.   Hark!   What sounds
Most awful from the East?

Cheers behind the scene.   Enter again ALOYS, EDWARD, *with several
   young peasants and herdsmen, all armed and equipped.* MARY
   retires to one side of the stage.)*

   Aloys.   Hurrah!   The men
Of Uri!

(HANNS IM HOF, *bearing the banner of Uri, appears on the summit of
   the hill.   He is followed by the warriors of that Canton.
   Every man bears on his left arm a red band, with a white
   Cross in the centre.   They all descend the path in single file,
   and come on the scene.   Whilst they are loudly welcomed by
   the men of Unterwalden,* EDWARD *approaches* MARY.)

   Edward. Mary, when, alive from war,
I shall return, and when the Holy Land
I shall have seen, I'll come again to speak

Of love to you, till then remember me!
Farewell!

Mary. My Lord, farewell!

Arnold.   Be welcome, Hanns,
My old and faithful friend! I feel ashamed
To see you on the march, whilst I, as yet
Am not prepared.

Hanns Im Hof. The land of Tell is first
To come, when freedom is in danger.

Aloys.   We,
The youth of Unterwald are ready too.

Edward. And I, a Bubenberg, will join your band,
For one for all, and all for one, we are
In Switzerland.

(*The tinkling of a little bell is heard. Two boys dressed in white
      gowns, followed by the priest* HENRY IM GRUND *in surplice,
      and bearing the* HOLY SACRAMENT *appear in the background.
      The whole crowd prostrate themselves in silence.*)

Henry.   From scenes of death I come.
To scenes of death you go. The Church of Christ
Bestows on all her children—care in life
Or death, and gives her blessing ever, when
For righteous cause they work, or live, or fight,
Or die.[2]

(*He makes the sign of the Cross three times over the kneeling crowd.*
      NICHOLAS OF THE FLUE *alone arises, and stands with hands
      and eyes uplifted to heaven.*)

5*

Nicholas. Almighty, everlasting GOD!
Be thou with them! Let Thine archangel walk,
With flaming sword, before the host that dares
Forever to uphold, defend the truth:
That MAN IS FREE! and tyrants shall not live,
Or thrive, within the bounds of Switzerland.

(*The curtain falls.*)

END OF ACT II.

ACT III.

***

The hall of the Senate in Berne. In the background arm-chairs in a semi circle, gradually rising from each side towards the centre, where, under a baldachin, is the seat of the Lord Provost, surmounted by the armorial escutcheon of Berne. A desk covered with green velvet, edged with golden fringes, before it. A bar separates the space, occupied by the seats of the Senate, from the foreground Within the semi-circle, three writing desks.

At the rising of the curtain the thunder of cannon is heard from the distance, amidst the tolling of bells. This continues at intervals during the whole scene. In the foreground of the hall, seats are placed on each side.

Enter HANNS WALDMANN, JOHN VON HALLWYL, LOUIS, Count of Gruyères, all in armor.

Waldmann. The Senate tarries long to meet.
    'Tis time
To know what shall be done. If not relieved,
I fear for Morat.

    Von Hallwyl. Never I, as long
As Bubenberg is there alive. I know

The man.   Two thousand there with him have kept
The town 'gainst sixty thousand, now for ten
Or eleven days.
Von Gruyères   The walls are undermined,
They say, the towers shot to atoms all.
   Von Hallwyl. In Bubenberg, there still remains a
     wall,
A massive wall—himself.

(*Cheers behind the scene.   The Uri horn is heard.   Enters* HANNS IM
HOF.)

   Waldmann.   Be welcome, friend!
My Lords, personified, in one most brave,
The land of Tell is here.
   Im Hof.   Confederates
In need will find the men of Uri true
To death.
   Waldmann. And Zürich not yet here!   I begged,
Besought my countrymen to hasten.   Cheers
Again!   Perhaps at last!

(*Enter* ARNOLD IM GRUND, PAUL ENNENTACHER, *and* CASPAR VON
HERTENSTEIN.)

              Ah, no! not they!
'Tis Unterwalden and Lucerne must take
The rank before my native town,
   Von Hertenstein.   My friend
Most worthy, rains and muddy roads have much
Detained us all.   A longer march than we

Your countrymen will have.   But hush ! I hear
The signal bell.   The Senate comes.

*(Enter first two sergeants-at-arms in long cloaks, half red, half black
One bears a sceptre of solid silver, the other a civic crown,
which both are placed on the desk of the Lord Provost.   The
sergeants-at-arms take position at each extremity of the semi-
circle.   Then enter* NICHOLAS VON SCHARNACHTHAL, *Lord
Provost;* WILLIAM VON DIESSBACH, *and* PETERMANN VON WA-
BERN, *ex-Lords Provost;* RUDOLPH VON ERLACH, *and the re-
maining Senators, all dressed in black, with swords at their
sides.   They take their seats, the Lord Provost that in the
centre, under the baldachin.   The chancellor and two secre-
taries occupy places within the semi-circle.*

Waldmann. (Aside to Von Hallwyl.)   How grave,
How dignified your rulers look !   Like kings
They sit on thrones, with calm and undisturbed
Expression, whilst the thund'ring cannon roars.
How I should like to see this royal mien
In Zürich's councils too!
Von Hallwyl.   My Lord Provost
Arises.   Silence now must reign around.
*Von Scharnachthal. (Lifting the sceptre with his
right hand, at which sign all the Senators rise and
uncover.)*
        In GOD ALMIGHTY's name !
All the Senators.   Amen !
Von Scharnachthal.   Provost
And Senate of the Commonwealth of Berne,
In council here assembled, have resolved :

Whereas His Highness most serene, the Duke
Of Burgundy, hath come again, with force
Invaded Berne's hereditary lands,
And now is laying siege around the town
Of Morat; since the forces we ourselves
Have called to arms are in the field, and all
Confederates and allies shall be here
To-day, we have resolved now to appoint
Of chief commanders three most valiant knights
Whom, summoned here, my Lords, you see before
You.   Well beloved and known by all at home
And feared abroad they are.   And since in war
Like this, where Berne is most exposed, 'tis meet
That Berne should be the first to march, and thus
My Lord von Hallwyl here is called to lead
The van; my Lord Hanns Waldmann, Zürich's pride,
The main ; my Lord von Hertenstein the rear.

(Noise and cheers behind the scene.   Drums and trumpets are heard
 Enter HANNS LANDENBERG, ULRIC VON HOHENSAX, PETER ROT,
 WILLIAM HERTER, FOSTER *of Bienne, Count* LOUIS OF OETTINGEN
 Count OSWALD OF THIRSTEIN.

 Waldmann. (*Shaking hands cordially with Landenberg.*)
My Lords, most thankful for the honor high
Conferred on me, I can your Lordships now
Inform, that Zürich's force hath come in full.

 Landenberg.   Three thousand men, and Sargans,
  Thurgovy,
With us.

Von Hohensax. From Argovy, my Lords, I bring
Two thousand.

Peter Rot.   Basil, two thousand too, and horse
One hundred.

Foster.   Bienne is here.

Von Hallwyl.   As ever, Bienne
And Berne are one.

William Herter.   And Strasburgh sends of horse
Three hundred, cannons twelve, and marksmen still
Four hundred.

Von Hallwyl. Berne, my Lord, hath in the field
Eight thousand, all most anxious for the word
To march.

Von Scharnachthal. The order will be issued now.
To-night the march begins.

(*Cheers outside. Music, drums. Enters* RENÉ, *Duke of Lorraine.*
All the Senators rise. Those on the foreground give way to
the Duke, who comes to the centre, before the railing. The
Senators resume their seats.)

René.   Magnificent,
Most gracious Lords of Berne :[1] magnanimous
In all your deeds, in virtues great, and just,
Defenders of oppressed : an exile here
I come, of country, home, estate deprived
By Charles, your foe and mine.   In vain I have
Besought for help His Majesty, the King
Of France.   I come to you and humbly ask,
Your Lordships may most graciously allow

That I, with few who have remained to me
Yet faithful from Lorraine, may join your host.

 Von Scharnachthal. Your Highness most serene,
  if we Provost
Express the thanks of Berne for honor, such
As offered here, we hope, my Lords, we shall
But shape, in words, the Senate's sentiment
Unanimous.

(All the Senators bow in acquiescence.)

   With sorrow deep, we all
Have heard, how arbitrary hands have seized
The realms of fair Lorraine, without a just
Apparent cause.

 Von Erlach. Your Lordships' leave! I move,
His Highness to appoint to a command.

 Von Scharnachthal. The chief commanders have
  been named. It is
Their privilege, their own, chiefs to appoint
To their divisions.

 Von Hallwyl. Right in time, my Lords,
This offer comes. His Highness in the van
May take the third division. First of all
The men of Forest Cantons, Entlibuch
And Oberland, commands the chief of Schwytz,
Of Schwytz renowned, the heart of Switzerland.
And since His Highness, Archduke Sigismond
Of Austria, now in peace and friendship bound

To us, forgetful of all feuds of yore,
Between the house of Habsburgh and ourselves,
Hath sent the valiant Count of Thierstein here,
With force most unexpected, cavalry
Adapted well to act on ground, like that
Near Morat, he the horsemen may command.
I hope my Lords approve of this design.
    Von Scharnachthal. No better man hath Berne to
      send than him,
The hero who, with Hunyad, Corvin,
Podiebrad abroad, on Granson's field
At home, hath won undying fame.   My Lord
Von Hallwyl, we, the Senate trust in you.
But furthermore we are instructed, now
To read to all the chiefs assembled here,
What from Lucerne, the Diet of the land
Hath sent to be addressed to all the troops.
The delegates of the eternal league
Of Uri, Schwytz, and Unterwald, Lucerne,
And Zürich, Glaris, Zug, and Berne, have passed
The ordinance, to wit: " From hence no more
" Shall volunteers irregular be left
" To go to war without command.   The chiefs
" Must be obeyed by all, and every one
" Goes in the field in armor which, nor day
" Nor night he is to leave, as long as lasts
" The war.   All private feuds and riots wild,
" By penalty of death, we here forbid;
6

" And gambling, swearing, cursing, idle noise
" Shall not be suffered in the field.   No man
" Shall leave the ranks without permission.   Each
" In order goes against the foe, a word
" To GOD, and then, with open eye and arm
" Unwearied, slays as many as he can.
" No captives are desired.   Whoever turns
" To fly is slain by those behind him.   Those
" Attempting to desert, for perjury
" With death will be rewarded.   Helpless age
" Or sex let none molest!   Let none forget
" In church or priest to honor GOD, the Judge
" Of war!   No mill shall be destroyed.   The van
" Shall burn no place.   Provision there the rear
" May find.   In order to prevent dispute
" And quarrels all, no booty shall be touched
" Before the victory is won, and then
" Authorities, with fairness, will divide
" The spoil."[2]   Such is the law, on oath to be
Observed by all.

    A Sergeant-at-arms. Your leave, my Lord Provost:
A messenger from Morat hath arrived
With news important,

    Von Scharnachthal. Let him come before
The Senate!

(Enters ALOYS, covered with dust.)

    What, the herdsman knight! my Lords:

Arise! Of Unterwalden's sons you see
The bravest here.

(All the Senators rise, and look with an admiring smile on ALOYS.*)*

Aloys. My Lords, this message will
Excuse, I hope, appearance so unfit
As mine, before a council so august,
Magnificent, as that of Berne.

(He gives a letter to the sergeant-at-arms, who presents it to the Lord
Provost.)

Arnold. (*In a low voice, to Aloys.*) My son,
Be welcome!

Von Hallwyl. Noble boy! As soon as we
Have finished here, you come with me. You are
This day in Berne my guest. A friend of your's
Is at my house; most gladly she will see
You there. To-night we march.

Von Scharnachthal. Your Lordships' leave!
This letter comes from valiant Bubenberg
Himself. (*Reads.*) " As long as there a vein within
Us lives, not one of us will yield. I send
In haste these lines to you, my Lord Provost.
The messenger, your Lordship, knows. He can
Relate, in words, what time will not allow
To write."
                        (*To* ALOYS.)

My brave Sir herdsman knight, will please
Inform us all, what circumstance hath brought
Him here.

Aloys. My Lords, excuse a herdsman's simple
    speech!
Affairs in Morat gloomily would look,
If Lord von Bubenberg did not infuse
In every man his own heroic mind;
For yesterday again the town sustained
A storm terrific.   Hell itself appeared
In rage to have unchained its demons all,
From South, from East, from West, against the meek
But faithful town.   As if by earthquake shocked—
The walls and houses trembled.   Shot on shot
Like hail around us fell.   A breach was made.
The enemy with shouts of joy upon
It rushed, but met a living fence he could
Not climb.   With loss of seven hundred men
He was repulsed.   O'er ditches filled with brush,
With ladders came the foe, and crowd on crowd
Arrived, with yells infernal, tried to scale
The walls.   In vain!   My Lord Commander seemed
To be in every place at once, with words
Of Fatherland and death for liberty
Inspiring every soul; and thus the third
Attempt to storm the town was baffled too;
At least a thousand enemies fell in this
Assault, and Morat still is standing.   Hard,
Indeed, the press is now upon it.   Day
And night the men must work——
  Von Scharnachthal.   Relief will go
To-night.

(*Taking the sword from the table.*)

And now in GOD ALMIGHTY's name!
We take, unsheathe the swords and lift them up
And swear, that we, like one, will all, for GOD
And country fight, avenge injustice done.
Oh, GOD! in mercy help us to defend
Our land, as Thou hast done so oft before!

(*All the Senators, with swords uplifted, stand in solemn silence at their places. The rays of the setting sun fall upon the scene.*)

SCENE II.

A garden behind the mansion of JOHN VON HALLWYL, on Younker street, in Berne. Enter JULIA VON BUBENBERG and RENÉ, Duke of Lorraine.

Julia. And thus, Your Highness says, they rose to
    greet
The herdsman knight?
René.   The herdsman king, his name
Should be. Though modest, like a king he stood
'Midst kings, his equals, spake in language terse,
Precise, as orator of nature. All
The Senate listened, spell-bound, to his tale.
How proud, my Lady, there would you have been,
To hear him speak of his commander, Lord
Von Bubenberg, your most illustrious sire!
Julia. And not a word of what he did himself.

6*

My brother writes that, when the breach was made
My father was the first to leap into
The hollow space. The largest gun of siege
Just glared him in the eye. The burning lunt
The master gunner lifted to the vent——
The herdsman's arrow pierced his heart, and thus
Was saved my father.

    René.   Strange it is! This youth
So modest, unassuming he appears
At first, but when by thought or feeling moved,
His eyes, like sparks of fire intense, assume
A lustre, dazzling him who dares to meet
His look. A mystic spell you feel. Methinks
The eye of Cæsar must have been like his.

    Julia. The freeman's eye! It beams of love of
        home,
Of Fatherland and liberty.

    René.   Alas!
Of Fatherland I am deprived. My own,
My beautiful Lorraine I dare to see
No more!

    Julia. Your Highness still may hope. Perhaps
To-morrow's day will show, what doom awaits,
Unjust, unreined ambition, thirst of power.

    René. Oh, noble lady, fit to wear a crown!
What gratitude I owe to you for all
The kind regards, the pleading of my cause
Before your mighty rulers! Words in vain

Would dare to tell, express, what feels my heart
For you.   Alas! I have my crown no more.

Julia. Your Highness may be sure, I feel with deep
Regret your loss of country.

René.   Pity moves
Forever woman's heart for others' woe.

Julia. Your Highness, pity——why?

René.   I dare not hope
For more, but if I had my crown, my land,
To you, most noble lady, would I be
So bold to offer all——

Julia. (*Starting with surprise.*)   Your Highness!

René.   Crown——
With heart and hand.

Julia.   Your Highness most serene:
Indeed, I feel surprised at words so strange,
And ill prepared to answer compliment
So flatt'ring, honorable——

René.   Could I dare
To hope?

Julia. Your Highness' friend sincere I am,
Shall ever be, but——love—

René.   You do not feel
For me.   I read it in your eye.   I know
My fate, farewell!

(*Exit* JULIA.)

                 Farewell, to country, home!
Farewell to hope, to love!   Oh, bitter pang

Of all the worst to say—farewell to love!
To plant a heavenly image in the heart,
Adorn with fancy's colors all its charms;
To dream by day and night about the fair
And lovely form, that, like a fairy, haunts
The chambers of the soul;—to idolize
That object more beloved than self, than all
The world; to concentrate your feelings, thoughts,
Ambition's wishes, aspirations high
On her you love—and then to be compelled
To tear away that image from the heart:
What torture! Bleeding roots in vain resist
The grasp of hands that snatch from you the plant
So fondly cultured. All the universe
Becomes a vacuum, dark, immense, without
A sun, a star, within the soul.
                                 Farewell
To love! Unfortunate René! Unmanned
I sink beneath the blows of fate. Oh life:
What burden!

(Music in the distance playing a martial air.)

            Hark! am I myself no more?
Have I forgot Lorraine? Ah, no! To thee
My country, still I owe a debt. I must
Avenge thy wrongs, deliver thee from chains.
One goal at least I have attained: I dare
To meet in arms the tyrant of my land.

Let private grief be hushed for my Lorraine,
Now whole to her, and all for her—Lorraine!

[*Exit.*]

(*Enters* JULIA.)

Julia. He's gone. 'Twas well I left. I could not
    trust
Myself. Poor Duke, so noble, handsome, still
So young, unfortunate, bereft of all
He loves! I felt my heart in pity yield,
And yet——

(*Enter* JOHN VON HALLWYL *and* ALOYS, *in armor, but without helmets.*)

Von Hallwyl. My cousin look! At last I have
Prevailed on him to take the armor, sword
And spurs, becoming knights. The name he will
Not take. How do you like the change?
Julia.   I see
No change but garments mere.
Von Hallwyl.   You know I have
Appointed him my aid de camp.

(*Enters a page.*)

Page.   My Lord
Von Hertenstein is waiting in the hall
For orders.
Von Hallwyl. Well, I leave my friend with you,
My cousin.

[*Exit.*]

Julia.   Thus again you have refused
The title you so well deserve?

Aloys.   I do
Not know my name, my origin as yet.

Julia. But you have won a name, a noble one.
The house of Bubenberg, with justice, calls
You now its tutelary knight.   You saved
At first my brother's, then my father's life.
What can I do for you?

Aloys.   A lovely smile
From you, most gracious lady, is reward
Sufficient for the little I have done.

Julia. There is a tone of sadness in your voice
Which speaks of silent grief.   You left a home,
A beauteous one, my brother says.   Is there,
Perhaps, a being whom your heart regrets?
Who is that lovely Mary?

Aloys.   Mary—why?
My sister.

Julia.   She your real sister?

Aloys.   No!
But such she is to me.

Julia.   I am your friend.
But tell me, do you love her?

Aloys.   Mary? yes,
Most dearly as a sister who, from years
Of childhood was my playmate.   Sweet hath been
To me her friendship.   Radiant beams her smiles

Have cast upon the morning of my life.
'She is as gentle as a dove, so mild,
So modest, pious, pure, and yet so firm
In her resolve. She hath her quiet ways,
A mind well cultured with her country's lore,
A heart most tender, ever ready to
Assist the ones in need. She is beloved
By all—the angel of the house.

   Julia. (*Aside.*)   I fear
My brother hath in him a rival. (*Aloud.*) **Then**
You feel most happy in your home ?

   Aloys.   Alas !
That home is not my own. I feel I am
A stranger there 'midst strangers, kind to me,
'Tis true.

   Julia. You never loved ?

   Aloys.   Alas ! I dare
Not love !

   Julia. You dare not love ? The man who **dares,**
With lion heart, to meet the foe, who, like
A king before the Senate stood, the man
Of whom our heroes all with high respect
And admiration speak, yet dares not love ?

   Aloys. My Lady, please forgive ! I feel so **sad**
In touching themes like this. I love—but love
In vain. The one I love is far, too far,
Above myself.

   Julia.   In Unterwalden ?

Aloys.   No!

Julia. Then where is she?

Aloys.   I dare not tell.

Julia.   Not tell
To me, your friend?

Aloys.   To you; oh, no!   I could
Not dare to be so bold to lift my eyes——
So high!   Excuse my words!   I do not know
What next may yet escape my lips.   I must
Depart.   My heart will break.

Julia.   But stay!   You have
Refused to kneel before my Lord Provost;
Will you refuse to wear this scarf I wrought
For you?   If not—then kneel that I may place
It on your shoulder, with my hand.   The words,
In gold embroidered here, shall be your own
Device from hence fore'er : *Remember me!*

Aloys. Remember you?   Could I behold you once
And then forget you ever?

Julia.   Kneel, my knight!

(ALOYS *kneels down.*)

My colors you shall wear, the white and blue,
The white of innocence and purity
The emblem,—blue, of love eternal.

Aloys.   Love!
Can this be true?   Oh, should I dare to hope,
Aspire——Is this a dream?

Julia.   Arise, and draw
The sword!

Aloys. (*Arising, and unsheathing his sword.*)
          For GOD, my country, and——

Julia.   For whom?

Aloys. For you!

Julia.   For GOD, your country, and for me,
Your own forever, Julia!

SCENE III.

The street of the Cross, in Berne. Night. The houses are all
illuminated. Tables covered with all kinds of refreshments are set
at each side of the street. Women of all classes wait on the march-
ing troops. In the background the council hall; a roofed piazza in
front of it, with stairs ascending on both sides from the street.
JOHN VON HALLWYL, HANNS WALDMANN, CASPAR VON HERTEN-
STEIN, RENÉ, Duke of Lorraine, the Lord Provost, and the Senate of
Berne are reviewing the troops from the piazza. As the latter march
over the scene, those of each Canton separately, they are cheered by
the multitude. Every Swiss warrior has a red band with a white
cross on the left arm.

WAR HYMN OF THE SWISS.

URI.

When foreign hosts invade the sacred soil
Of Liberty, the Uri horn is first,
With mighty blast, to call, from peaceful toil,
The sons of Tell, who all forever thirst
          To die or stand
          For Switzerland,
Their own, their own most glorious Fatherland.

SCHWYTZ.

The Cross of Schwytz appears in red to show: 3
Our fathers bought us freedom with their blood.
The nation's heart with love will ever glow
For justice, right, and Schwytz will march, with GOD
>> To die or stand
>> For Switzerland,
Our own, our own beloved Fatherland.

UNTERWALDEN.

The key of Unterwalden shuts the gate 4
Of freedom's vales against the tyrant's hand.
The sons of Winkelried will share the fate
Of Liberty's defenders' faithful band,
>> Will die or stand
>> For Switzerland,
Their own, their own immortal Fatherland.

LUCERNE.

>> To the rescue,
>> To the rescue
>> Of the country we come.
>> From the mountain,
>> From the valley,
>> From the castle, the drum
Is calling the herdsman, the peasant, the knight,
To march to the field, for the country to fight.

ZURICH.

>> To the rescue,
>> To the rescue
>> Of the country we come.
>> From the hamlet,

From the Village,
From the city, the drum
Is rousing the burghers and artisans all
For the league, the eternal, to conquer or fall.

GLARIS.

Land of Glaris, show thy banner,
Naefels saw Victorious!
Fridolin, thy sainted patron,
Hence forever glorious, 5
There appears as thy protector,
Blessings calling from on high
On thy sons, to him devoted,
Ready for their homes to die.

ZUG.

Humbly comes the smallest Canton,
Least in size, not least in love
For the Fatherland, the common.
Like a meek, a modest dove
Zug appears to need protection
'Gainst her mighty neighbor's hand;
Still, with joy, her sons will ever
Come to fight for Switzerland.

BERNE.

Hail to the brothers arriving,
Berne in distress to defend!
Hail to the Cross, the beloved
Sign of the Swiss, on the band
Borne on the arm of the champion
When, for the league, in a war!

Hail to the lords and the peasants,
Coming from near and afar,
Here to assist in maintaining
Right for the home of the Free!
Nobles and peasants united,
Switzers forever will be!

CHORUS OF THE EIGHT CANTONS.

Yea—brothers, Switzers all, and true, as heretofore
We will be one, be one, be one forevermore!

(*The curtain falls.*)

END OF ACT III.

ACT IV.

Headquarters of CHARLES, Duke of Burgundy, before Morat. A chamber in the camp-house of the Duke. Time, June 22, 1476, one o'clock, A. M. OLIVIER DE LA MARCHE is seen placing a richly gilt volume on a small table, before a magnificent camp-bed. Enters WILLIAM, Prince of Orange.

William.   What! so late,
And still the Duke hath not returned?
   Olivier.   He left
The tent, an hour ago, to take a last
Survey of outposts on the South.
   William.   The first
To rise, the last to rest, His Highness seems
Of matter formed, supernal, different
From other mortals.   Even whilst asleep
His mind appears to work, not to repose.
   Olivier. Yet all his cheerfulness of former times
Is gone.   That fatal day of Granson changed
His mood.   His confidence in self, his own

7*   77

Creative genius, there received a shock
That lamed the eagle's wings, and now in **vain**
He tries to soar to wonted spheres; but here
He comes! His face is flushed. His piercing **eye,**
In wrath and anger, seems to glow.

(*Enter* CHARLES, *Duke of Burgundy;* THOMAS, *Duke of Somerset,*
ANTHONY, CREVECOEUR, RUBEMPRÉ,)

Charles. (*Throwing himself on an arm-chair.*)
        'Tis past
Endurance! Here this petty town you can
Not take. If thus, in things so small, you fail,
What then must I expect in things of great
Import?
 Anthony. My liege and august brother knows,
That shot and men have not been spared.
 Charles.   It seems
Your shot is made of clay or dust, and all
Your men are soulless puppets.
 Anthony.   Morat's pierced
And shattered walls, and fallen towers speak,
In different terms, of all that hath been done.
What earthly power can sustain this town,
I cannot say.

(*Enters* COUNT CAMPOBASSO.)

Charles. I hope you bring at last
The answer I expect, from him I once
With favors showered, whom, in friendship **bound**

To me, I always thought.   What message sends,
By flag of truce, my valiant Bubenberg?
Will he surrender?

    Campobasso.   No, my liege! he begs
Your Highness to remember but the word——
    Charles. What word?
    Campobasso.   Thermopylæ!
    Charles.   Leonidas.—
He wants to play.   By Sainted George! he shall
Not have the chance.   I know the stuff of which
That man is made.   In purpose firm as rocks,
I do regret to have his like against me.   Since
I learned that he, my former friend, commands
The town, I comprehend, the task is great,
Immense, to crush a mind like his.   My name
Shall not, with that of Xerxes, go to times
To come.   I wish for contest fair.   The boors
Of Berne who dare to call themselves the lords,
I long to humble, crush, avenge the foul
Disgrace my fright'ned troops for once did bring
On me and my, till then, unconquered arms.
But Bubenberg I wish to spare.   We need
Pursue the siege no more.   I am informed,
The forces of the Swiss are on the march.
In fair and open field, I wish to meet—
Defeat them.   Tricks of cunning I despise.
The Lion of Bourgogne will not to ruse
Ignoble condescend.

Anthony.   My liege, forgive
My boldness!   Well it would have been, I think,
To act, with sentiment so noble, fair,
Towards that brave and unsuspecting band
Surrend'ring Granson's castle, on the word
Of promise given by——

Charles. (*Furious.*)   Who dares to speak
Of things like these, remind me of mistakes
I did not make?   The garrison was hung,
As I had ordered; none had right to grant
A pardon, in my name.

Anthony.   'Twas Ronchant's deed,
I know.   He trusted in Your Highness' great
And gen'rous mind.

Campobasso.   My liege most high was right
To make example of that stubborn band,
And show the boors, what fate awaits them all,
If they will dare to vex the lion proud.

Anthony. The flatt'rer's honeyed tongue I will
          not use.
I do regret for fair Burgundy's name,
The act that hath exasperated all
Our foes to fight with lion's wrath.

Campobasso.   My Lord
Would be, perhaps, a little more correct
In saying, that they fight like bears—the beasts
Of Berne.

Anthony. Like wounded bears, they fought, indeed,

Charles.　　　　　I know your lore.
'Tis not for speech like this, I called you here.
But tell me, when and where you saw my own,
My guardian star, of late?

Astradamus.　　　　　When last I saw
It—there it was on zenith's height, eclipsed
In brilliancy the stars of rulers all.
In vain a neb'lous circle tried to dim
Its lustre for a time,

Charles.　　　　　By Sainted George!
It never shall! Before another sun
Hath set, its brightness shall eclipse the stars
Of all that, in my age, have dared to cross
My path.

Astradamus. I hope it will be so, but still,
My liege, remember what I said: *Astra*
Regunt homines, sed regit astra
Deus!

Charles. You may withdraw! 'Tis all I wished
To know of you.

(*Exit* Astradamus.)

The old adage! When man
Becomes perplexed in thoughts and problems deep,
He cannot solve—then will he talk of God.
Is there a God? Oh, question most profound!
Portentous thought that often will impede
My greatest schemes! If what the priests have
　　taught

8

Me, from my youth, be true, and CHRIST be GOD,
Then who shall have a chance more bright than I
Before that GOD? Is there a land in which
His temples are as splendid as in mine?
Have I not prayed, and prayed, as much as do
His priests the most devout, the Office read,
And Mass attended every day? Have I
Not vowed to free the Holy Land, as soon
As all my foes, here in the West, should be
Subdued? Have I not honored Church and priest,
And Saints, and holy relics? Where is found
A land with greater justice ruled than mine?
Have I oppressed my subjects? No! To all—
The rich, the poor, I wish to be a friend,
A father. Why that GOD should be against
Myself, I cannot understand. My wealth
I have bestowed to deck His shrines with all
The costliest tissues, jewels. Who will find,
In royal chapels, ostensorium
Like mine?

(*After a pause.*)

And yet, in spite of all this, doubt,
Most cruel doubt, will oft besiege my mind.
I see so much of falsehood, mixed with all
That wears religious colors. Pride, intrigue,
And lust, hypocrisy, and love of gain,
Are hidden under cloaks most sacred. Why—

If there be such a GOD, who hateth sin,
Doth He allow His own defenders, priests,
Belie His law and precepts by their lives?
I've ponder'd, ponder'd over this so oft,
And other problems, still more difficult,
And all the pang of thinking leaves me here,
In mist of darkness.

     Man—for what design
Mysterious hath he been created? Who
Can tell? Might he not be, as sages said,
Of old—himself a part of what the priest
Is calling GOD? Am I a God?

        But truce
To metaphysic musing now! I need
Some rest, some sleep. Whate'er I am, I am
Myself alone in species; trust I must
Alone in force within myself. My mind
I must infuse into my host, that will,
That conquering strength which Cæsar, Hannibal,
And Alexander would infuse into
Their legions. Who shall dare to cope with me?

(*He lies down and falls asleep. The scene darkens. The tapestry, in
the background, is slowly withdrawn, and, in a tableau, is
shown*—

THE DREAM OF CHARLES THE BOLD.

(*The forest of Ranft is seen through a rosy mist. NICHOLAS OF THE
FLUE, MARY, and LILY are kneeling before a simple wooden
Cross, erected before the hermitage. The orchestra accompa-*

nies, in a slow and solemn symphony, the chanting of the prayers.)

Lily.   Redeemer mine
In Heav'n above,
Before Thy sign
Of bounteous love,
At break of day,
I call on Thee,
And humbly pray,
Preserve to. me
A father's life!
With mighty hand,
In bloody strife,
My native land
Protect against
A haughty foe,
By pride incensed,
To strike the blow
Of Death to all
Who will defend,
At Freedom's call,
My Fatherland!

Mary.   Before Thy throne
We sink in dust,
Oh, GOD! Alone
In Thee we trust.
The foe may boast,

With haughty pride,
Of all his host:
We pray—abide
With us, oh, GOD!
As sinners—we
Deserve the rod,
But still to Thee,
In anguish—wo,
We fly to pray:
In grace bestow
Thy help this day
On those who go,
With sword in hand,
Against the foe
Of Switzerland!

Nicholas of the Flue. (Arising with hands uplifted and turning his eyes on Charles.)

Thus saith the LORD
Of Hosts, by all
In Heav'n adored:
The proud will fall
And lose his throne;
Like grass his lines,
They shall be mown.
Before My shrines
The humble, meek
The trusting child

8*

That comes to seek
A father mild—
Alone I will
Exalt and hear.
My Mercy still
On those that fear
My name, and keep
My will—My Law
In rev'rence deep,
In holy awe—
I will impart,
Bestow my grace.
THE PURE IN HEART
SHALL SEE MY FACE !

(*End of the dream.*)

Charles. (*Awakening, rises from his couch, looks haggardly around, and staggers over the scene.*)

A child, a woman, and a hermit old !
Is this a dream of warning purport, or
A whim of evil spirits, used to scare
A weak and superstitious coward ?   Ah !
You missed your mark.   And yet this chant so weird,
In mournful echoes lingers in my soul.
Away with vain forebodings !   Charles : art thou
A child ?

(*He rings a bell. A page appears with a small package in his hand.*)

A cup of wine!   How is the night?

Page. Your Highness most serene, the day begins
To dawn.   It raineth still.

Charles.   What have you here?

Page. The messenger from Ghent hath brought—

Charles.   From Ghent?
'Tis from the Duchess, I suppose——

(*Exit page. Breaking open the package, and taking out a miniature
richly incased in jewels.*)

Ah, no!

(*Kissing the miniature.*)

My child, my darling Mary, pride of all
Bourgogne!   What sweet surprise!   How beautiful!
How like herself!   A noble prize for which
Tarent, Savoy, and Austria, England, France—
Are vieing with each other, who may win
Thy heart and hand, now Europe's richest boon.

(*Re-enters the page, and presents a golden cup to the Duke, who
drinks,*)

Charles. (*To the page.*)
'Tis time my generals should meet.   You may
To council call them here.

(*Exit page.* CHARLES *opens a letter and reads :*)

" Illustrious sire

"And most beloved father!   Here I send

"Your faithful daughter's likeness, which, I hope,
"You will be pleased to see. I think of you,
"Dear father, day and night, and wish to be
"Forever at your side. Oh, that I might
"Again behold you once at Dijon's court!
"I felt so happy there with you. Alas!
"That war should tear you from your child, **and**
      keep
"My heart in constant fear for you! I wish
"You could have shunned this strife with Switzer-
      land.
" A dream I had, some nights ago, hath filled
"My soul with strange and dark presentiment.
"I saw a child, a recluse old and feeble, with
" A youthful virgin pray before a Cross
"Against my own beloved father."——
                              What!
This dream, the very one I had myself!
Is then the world of spirits, too, in league
Against my house?   My child, my lovely child,
My only true devoted friend, must thou
With fancies strange in slumbers be disturbed?
I'll show to-day that dreams will but deceive
The ones that have no faith in self.
                              And yet,
I wish, my child, that thou wert here with me.
Thy presence, like a soothing breeze, to calm
Will ever bring the stormy waves within

My soul, when I am crossed, in lofty schemes,
By dull and common-place, or stubborn minds.
But here my generals come.   I must defer
The reading of thy dear epistle, child !
To moments of repose.

(*Enter* ANTHONY, THOMAS, *Duke of Somerset;* WILLIAM, *Prince of Orange;* CREVECOEUR, CAMPOBASSO, OLIVIER DE LA MARCHE.)

                              What prospect now
Have we for meeting with the foe to-day ?
Are things prepared as I have ordered ?
     Anthony.   Yes,
My liege.   The Count of Romont holds with force
The western shore- of Morat's lake, and will
Arrive in time to fall upon the right,
The weakest flank the foe hath to oppose.
     Charles. 'Tis one advantage we shall have this time·
The foe will be obliged to come on plain,
On even ground, and not, according to
His custom, fight in narrow defile, where,
With one to three of us, he dared to brave
My valiant host.
     Somerset.   And cavalry will here,
At least, now be of some avail.   I think
The foe is weak in horse.
     Campobasso.   He hath of them
A handsome number, led, I learned, by Count
Von Thierstein, Duke René, and——

Charles.   What, the boy
Lorraine, is he with them?
    Campobasso.   The same, my liege.
    Charles. The houses Anjou, Habsburgh, and the
      boors
Of Berne: what combination strange! But do
You know what force, in numbers, they can bring,
To bear upon our own?
    Anthony.   I cannot say.
No gold can buy the meanest churl to act
As spy.
    Campobasso. A scout, of Lombardy, by birth,
But versed in German tongue, whom I had sent
In peasant's garb to Berne but yesterday,
Hath just returned. He thinks the foe must be
At least some thirty thousand strong.
    Charles.   The odds
Are then for us; and now, my Lords, let all
Be done as I have ordered! When the Swiss
Appear, receive them well with shot! A hedge
Towards the south will hide, protect our men.
The infantry, in columns deep and dense,
Will stand behind, in order to repel
The foes, if they should dare to come, advance
Up to the cannons' mouths. And now, though kings
And princes, boors and stars, and spirits, dreams—
May try to cast the darksome cloud of fear

Around the soul of Charles, their efforts shall
Be vain.   Bourgogne, forever live Bourgogne!
  All. Bourgogne, Bourgogne, forever live Bour-
    gogne!

  (*Music in the camp playing the national air of Burgundy.*)

SCENE II.

A forest on the summit of a hilly ridge, south of Morat.   The van
of the Swiss army on the right side, extending to the background.
To the left, in the distance, the tents of the Burgundian camp; and
beyond the latter the lake of Morat.

  VON HALLWYL surrounded by ALOYS, DUKE RENÉ, COUNT VON
THIERSTEIN, WILLIAM HERTER, and ARNOLD IM GRUND are in the
foreground.

  Von Hallwyl. (*Addressing the troops.*)
" Most valiant men, confederates in one
Eternal league united: there—before
You, are your brothers' murderers of Brie
And Granson.   They have cast the lot upon
Your land, your wives and children at Lausanne.
You wish revenge for this.   You see them there,
In numbers strong.   Remember well this day,
Confederates, this day—the same on which
A hundred thirty-seven years ago,
Our fathers met the foe on Laupen's field!
And, though in numbers less than he, their arms
United conquered all.   That GOD who gave
Them victory is still the same, and still

There breathes in you the same undaunted mind.
Let every one of you then fight, as if
The day's success, the commonwealth of all
Confederates, the weal of all he loves,
Were placed into his hands alone.   And now,
Oh, brothers! so that He who did assist
Our fathers may His help on us bestow,
Collect your inmost thoughts and let us pray!²"

(*All kneel down, and remain with arms outspread and eyes uplifted
during the prayer.   Von Hallwyl holds the standard of the
Confederacy (a white Greek cross in a red field) in his left hand.*

Von Hallwyl. Almighty everlasting God and Lord
Of hosts, eternal Judge of nations all:
Before Thy throne we here prostrate ourselves,
And humbly pray for help.   Without Thine arm
We can do naught, but Thou art mighty, strong,
And wilt assist Thy children in distress.
We trust in Thee, through Christ's redeeming death.
   Arnold Im Grund. Our Father, Thou who art in
       Heav'n above,
Most hallowed be Thy name!   Thy kingdom come!
Thy will be done on earth as it is done
In Heaven!   Give us this day our daily bread!
Forgive our sins, as we forgive to those
That sin against ourselves, and lead us not
Into temptation, but deliver us
From evil!   Amen!
   All.   Amen!

(The sun breaks through the clouds at this moment.)

Von Hallwyl.   Now arise!
Arise! You see that GOD Himself will light
Us on the way. Remember now your wives
And children! Youths of Switzerland: will you
Allow that foreign arms should e'er possess
The ones you love?

(They all arise and advance in a dense line. The cannon begins to roar in the distance. Music playing martial airs. During the noise, shouts, cheers, and tumult of the battle, the scene changes.)

SCENE III.

The interior of the great Minster of St. Vincent, in Berne. Night. The church is crowded by women, children, and decrepit old men, all on their knees. A black curtain is drawn between the Sanctuary and the congregation. A large, white Latin cross is seen on the curtain. Three priests, in white surplices, are kneeling before the railing, at the sides of which a few tapers are burning. The organ slowly accompanies the chant of the priests.

De profundis Domine:
Omnes ad Te hodie
Venimus clamantes.
Rex, Creator omnium
Angelorum, hominum:
Audi nos orantes!

9

Voces nostras non sperne,
Sancte Deus aeterne,
Judex nationum!
Tanto in periculo,
Dona nostro populo,
Vi precationum,
Et per Tuam gratiam,
Domine: victoriam,
Pacem diuturnam!
Regni Tui gloria,
Et Misericordia,
Sanctum Tuum nomen—
Semper sint perpetua,
Omnia per saecula
Saeculorum, Amen![3]

(A pause during which all remain in solemn silence.)

A single voice from the choir. Kyrie eleison!
Kyrie eleison!
Chorus.   Kyri-e
Eleison!

*(The dawn begins to break through the upper windows. Music is heard,
at first in the distance, then coming nearer and nearer. Shouts
of victory are heard from without.)*

Another voice from the choir.

Christe, Christe, eleison!

(Enter JOHN VON HALLWYL, ADRIAN VON BUBENBERG, NICHOLAS
VON SCHARNACHTHAL, HANNS WALDMANN, ALOYS, EDWARD

von Bubenberg, Arnold Im Grund, Rudolph von Erlach, Duke René, Caspar von Hertenstein, followed by the Senators of Berne and a crowd of soldiers, all walking with heads uncovered, through the middle aisle.   John von Hallwyl bears, in his right hand, the ducal standard of Burgundy. When the procession reaches the centre of the church, the curtain is slowly withdrawn from the Sanctuary, and the altar appears entirely illuminated.   All present prostrate themselves. Von Hallwyl advances towards the railing, and places the conquered banner at the foot of the altar.   One of the priests intones the " Gloria."   Above the Crucifix in the middle of the altar appear, in large, brilliant characters the words :

GLORIA IN EXCELSIS

DEO !

Whilst the choir chant the first part of the " Gloria in excelsis," the curtain falls.)

END OF ACT IV.

ACT V,

SCENE I.

The forest of Ranft. Before the hermitage of Nicholas of the Flue. Arnold Im Grund, Mary, Hanns Zumbrunnen of Uri, Dietrich Inderhalden of Schwytz, Henry Zelger, of Unterwalden.

Nicholas. Be welcome, friends, here in my solitude!

Arnold. We come to ask you for advice about
The welfare of the land.

Nicholas. What now? The land,
It is at peace at last. Your neighbors all,
The king of France, the Emperor, the Duke
Of proud Milan, the Duchess of Savoy,
They all with deep respect, and most of them
With fear, behold the valiant Switzer's League,
And Charles the Bold is now no more.

Arnold. He was
A noble foe. Indeed I grieved to hear,
With what an awful end he met at last;

9*

A fate that ought to teach forever all
Ambition's victims blind, that none do sit
So safe and firm on solid thrones, that stood
The storms of ages, yet may fall, decay,
And crumble into dust.

Nicholas.   Th' Almighty's see
Alone remains unmoved.   Before His throne,
His judgment seat, the nations all appear,
And onward pass into oblivion, if
Their hands are stained with guilt, injustice, **wrong,**
And blood untimely shed.   The end of Charles,
To princes not alone may teach, that thirst
For ruling power, once will bring disgrace
Upon their heads.

Arnold.   'Tis true we are at peace
With all around us.   Oh! that GOD would **grant**
We were at peace amongst ourselves.

Mary.   I fear,
The great success with which the Swiss have kept
Their foes at bay, for generations now,
Will fill their hearts with pride and vain conceit
That leadeth, soon or late, to deeds unjust.

Nicholas. I understand, contentions now **arise**
Amongst the Cantons all, about the spoils
The victory o'er Charles has thrown into   •
The Switzers' hands.

Arnold.   My Brother Claus speaks **well.**
I wish that all the booty, seized from Charles,

Were buried deep in Morat's lake, in which
His soldiers were engulphed. But now what can
Be done? Our youth are mad by thirst of gold.

Zumbrunnen. 'Tis not the only cause of wild dispute
Amongst the Cantons now; you know that oft,
When deputies from all the League would meet,
On council days to act, deliberate
On common weal, the Forest Lands would have
To feel the overbearing haughty airs
Of deputies from cities rich and proud.

Zelger. And often we, the simple herdsman, have
Been drawn, against our will and wish, into
The brawls and petty quarrels, which the lords
And burghers would incite amongst themselves.
'Tis hard for us, the founders of the League,
For Uri, Schwytz, and Unterwalden now,
To be dictated to by those who owe
Their strength to our assistance.

Inderhalden.   Neither have
The Forest Lands forgotten yet the vile
And shameful treachery of Zürich which,
For fifteen years, seceded from the League,
And warred against her brethren, joined their foes.

Nicholas. The past is gone. For this offence the
        pride
Of Zürich hath been humbled; but of late,
She acted nobly for the League with you.
When civil war is o'er, the sooner you

Forget, forgive the mutual wrongs, the more
You will enhance your bliss; the stronger will
Become the tie 'midst brothers reconciled.

  Zumbrunnen. The cities of Soleure and **Friburgh**
   now
Present themselves before the Diet of
The land, and humbly ask to be allowed
To join the Switzers' mighty League.
  Nicholas.   For you
Their warriors fought, on Morat's day.
  Inderhalden.   But Berne,
Lucerne and Zürich wildly claim for them
The right to be admitted. Still, methinks,
With reasons sound, the Forest Lands object
To see so many cities in the League.
  Zelger. The Forest Cantons, too, have been **refused**
The share they claim from conquered spoil. **In vain**
The Diet hath assembled, several times,
To bring about a friendly end to all
Dispute. The cities will not yield. What shall
Become of us, I do not know.
  Nicholas.   I hope
That envy, greedy selfishness, and mean
Desire of wealth will nevermore succeed
In bringing ruin on the sacred League.
My worthy friends must trust in GOD, and **pray**
That He may guide them on their duty's path.

Zumbrunnen, Inderhalden, and Zelger.
We will, most worthy Brother Claus.
Arnold. And ask
To be remembered in your pray'rs. Farewell!

(*Exeunt all but* MARY, *who looks somewhat embarrassed.*)

Nicholas. What ails my child? This sadness I've
   observed
For weeks. Thou art not well; thy face is pale,
Thy eyes are red, as if from weeping. Speak
To me, my child!
Mary. (*Bursting into tears.*) Oh, father, can I help
It, being much alarmed? Two years have now
Elapsed since Aloys and——
Nicholas. Edward, Lord
Von Bubenberg, have gone to Palestine.
Mary. And now for thirteen months, no news hath
   come.
Nicholas. Thou art mistaken, child. Be cheerful!
   Both
Will soon return. A pilgrim from the East
Was here but yesterday. He saw them both,
And sound in health, in Venice safely land.
Mary. Oh, thanks, my worthy father! GOD be
   praised!
They did not fall, as I have feared, into
A corsair's hands.
Nicholas. Indeed, myself, I much

Rejoice at their return.   They will be rich
In pious lore from Holy Land.   'Twas well
For them to have escaped from passions fierce,
Aroused within the breasts of Switzers now,
By love of plunder, envy, avarice,
Which, like a plague, are threatening the land.

   Mary. Oh! father, is it true, and must it come
To pass?   Is there no help?   Is Switzerland
To be a prey to fell dissension?

   Nicholas.   Child!
I hope it not.   May GOD ALMIGHTY guide—
Direct our rulers' hearts!

   Mary.   Oh, father! pray
To GOD for us, for this, our dearest home,
Our Fatherland!

   Nicholas.   I will, my child, do thou
The same!

                         [*Exeunt.*]

SCENE II.

A chamber in the mansion of BUBENBERG, in Berne.   ADRIAN is
reclining on a large arm-chair; JULIA, kneeling at his side, and hold-
ing one of his hands in hers.

   Julia. My father, speak! I cannot bear
Suspense.   Is there no hope?

   Adrian.   My child, I fear
My days are number'd.

   Julia.   No! it cannot be.

You are not old.   You must, you will get well
Again.

Adrian. Alas! for thee, my daughter, I
Would gladly wish it could be thus.   I am
Not old in years, and yet how old in sad
Experience, disappointment's bitter pangs!
Ingratitude hath been my share for all
I've done.   I'm tired of the world, with all
Its vain delusive show, pretence and base
Hypocrisy.

Julia.   My father, please be calm!
'Tis not for self that you have lived and worked.
Your country, Berne, the whole of Switzerland,
Will ever bless your name, uphold your high,
Your noble, matchless sacrifice of self   .
Unto her youth, in future days, and stir
Their souls, with patriotic zeal and flame,
To follow your example.

Adrian.   Glory, fame,
Renown: what sounds so hollow, empty on
The verge of dark eternity!   My child,
Disturb me not, in time so solemn, now,
With words of vain, self-glorious praise.   I have
Confessed, and am prepared to die.   Oh, that
My son were here, my blessing to receive!

Julia. I must beseech you, father, banish from
Your mind the mournful thought of death!
You still may live for years.   The vigor of

Your frame is, surely, not yet gone.   Oh! let
Me cheer you up again!

(*A knock at the door is heard;* JULIA *arises; enter* JOHN VON HALL-
WYL.)

Adrian.   So soon, my friend?
Von Hallwyl. I heard but now, you sent for me.
      I came
At once.
Adrian. My child, I wish to see my friend
Alone.
Julia. I will withdraw.

(*Exit.*)

Adrian.   I sent for you.
I do not wish my child should ever know
The secret of my talk, and yet——
      Von Hallwyl.   What now?
You hesitate——
Adrian.   You always were my friend.
I will confess to you, what heavy weight
Is on my heart.
      Von Hallwyl. Your confidence is dear
To me.
Adrian. I feel that death approaches me.
I should depart with ease, if I could leave
My children free from care.   Alas! it can
Not be.   My wealth is gone.   I am involved
In debt, and most of mine estate is now

Most heavily encumber'd.   War, expense
For travel, embassies, and want of care,
And gen'rous trust in others brought me down
To this.   My daughter loves a noble youth
You know.   She is betroth'd to him.   He soon
May now return and claim her hand.   Alas!

Von Hallwyl. What then, my friend?

Adrian.   The child of Bubenberg,
My child is portionless.   Her father's name
Will be disgraced.   He dies insolvent; more
Than this—the felon's doom awaits his last
Remains, his ashes——[1]

Von Hallwyl.   Never! no, this shall
Not be, as long as Berne will stand on her
Foundation.   All I have, I pledge for you.
Your daughter, leave unto my care!   The name
Of Bubenberg, the noblest name of Berne,
Shall still remain untarnished, and yourself
Repose within the vault of your renowned
Ancestors.

Adrian. Thanks to GOD!   I have not been
Mistaken in my friend.   My darling child
Will not to insult, suffering, be exposed.
My son will soon return from Palestine.
He hath a sword to carve his way; he is
A man, but Julia, my daughter——

Von Hallwyl.   Shall
Not want, shall be provided for.   Myself
10

I will adopt her.   Berne: what shame, disgrace
Woulds't thou deserve to let thy saviour's child,
Thy noblest ornament, be brought to ill !

   Adrian. Oh, GOD of mercy, thanks! for now I can
Depart in peace.   My friend, you have restored
To me the trust in man, in friendship true.
But oh! my pride is humbled into dust;
A Bubenberg—a beggar!

   Von Hallwyl.   No! I represent
But Berne, your country, which can never pay
The debt she owes to you.   I beg my friend
Not to alarm, but calm himself about
His children's future.   Now far different themes
I have to call your mind to ponder on.
Most serious news hath come this morning from
Lucerne.   The Forest Lands are raving mad
Against the cities.   Thus the Diet hath
Again adjourned, and met without success.

(*Enter* JULIA.)

   Julia. Forgive my interrupting you.   My Lords
Von Stein, von Erlach, and von Scharnachthal
Have come, and urgently request to see
You.

   Adrian. Now?

   Von Hallwyl. I know they come to ask for your
Advice about the country's weal.   Von Stein
Hath just returned this morning from Lucerne.

Adrian. Admit my Lords!

Julia. But, father, you are ill.
Their visit will excite you.

Adrian. Hush, my child!
In life or death—my country first!

(*Enter* PETERMANN VON STEIN, NICHOLAS VON SCHARNACHTHAL, *and*
RUDOLPH VON ERLACH.)

Von Erlach. Our eyes,
My Lord, are gladdened by the sight of you.

Von Scharnachthal. I hope you feel relieved from
fever's grasp.

Von Stein. The pride of Berne you are. Your life
is dear
To all her children.

Adrian. Thanks, my noble Lords!
What tidings from Lucerne?

Von Erlach. Most threat'ning for
The League.

Adrian. The League?

Von Stein. The Forest Cantons will
Not yield a single point. Their wrath against
Lucerne and Zürich, Berne, for daring to
Ally themselves with Friburgh and Soleure,
Hath swelled, increased to madness, rage. They say
That forming leagues, with lands or towns, is 'gainst
The covenant that binds the Cantons all.

Adrian. The Forest Lands, in fact, are clinging to

The letter's strictest sense.   We know it all:
The covenant of the eternal League
Was formed with this condition.

Von Stein.   What shall we
The cities, strongest in the League, shall we
The nobles, yield, submit to boors?

Adrian.   Is there
Another way?

Von Stein. The League may be dissolved.
We can secede.

Adrian   Secede, from what?

Von Stein.   The League!

Adrian. SECEDE! Oh, GOD! Is it for this that I
Have fought and bled? SECEDE! Oh, thought con-
    ceived
In Hell! Oh! heresy most damning!, What,
Dissolve the League eternal?   Who hath dared

(Arising from his seat.)

To utter words like these to me, a lord
Of Berne, a Bubenberg, a Switzer's son?

(He falls exhausted on his chair.)

Julia. For Heaven's sake! You kill my father
    thus.

Von Stein. Forgive! I did not think it would
    affect
Him so.

Von Erlach. What shall the cities——

Adrian.   Yield—I say—
Submit to all to save the League! The boors—
You call them? Ah, the noble hearts that felt
And beat for us! And must it come to this,
That they should be despised and scorned, because
Their sturdy hands that fought for us, for Berne,
Must till the soil, in time of peace, to gain
Their daily bread! The boors? Are they not men
Like us, created with immortal souls,
To GOD accountable for all their deeds
And thoughts? Oh! friends, remember how con-
    tempt
For lowly caste hath brought the haughty down
Into the dust—remember Charles the Bold!

Von Stein. 'Tis not their calling we despise, but we
Object to be exposed to insult coarse
And language rude, their delegates did heap
Upon the courteous knights and noble lords
Who met with them in council. More than this,
Not we, but they, the Forest Lands, were first
To threaten with secession from the towns.

Adrian. No matter who they were that utter'd first
The word of treason to the League, they all
Deserve the nation's fullest curse. *The League!*
It must forever be preserved, and last
As long as yonder snow-capped mountains stand.

Von Hallwyl. The Forest Lands were founders of
    the League:
10*

For years they held at bay their foes, without
The help of Zürich, Berne, Lucerne.

   Von Stein.   Have not
Your fathers fought against them, too?   Methinks,
Your house hath sided long with Habsburgh——

   Von Hallwyl.   True!
But Hallwyl's scion learned to love, respect
The sterling virtues of the peasants in
The Forest Lands, their honest purpose, clear,
Straightforward way, in action and in thought.
I am their friend.

   Adrian.   And so am I.   They may
Be blunt in speech and obstinate in will;
But whosoever knows them well, will find
Their hearts as true as steel.

   Julia.   Oh, father, thanks!
I know you are your country's warmest friend;
I love to hear you speak of those to whom
We owe so much.

   Von Scharnachthal. We much regret that you
Are ill, my Lord.   Your power, influence
Amongst the Forest Lands is great.   Not one
Of us, the nobles here, would better suit
To undertake an embassy to all
The Forest Cantons.   You are loved, revered,
By herdsman and by peasant there, and might
To peaceful issue bring contentions all.
We are suspected.

Adrian.   You, suspected, why?

Von Scharnachthal. They cast reproach on us,
  because they think
Or fancy, that the nobles ever look
With supercilious contempt upon
Their rustic manners, customs,

Adrian.   Well! perhaps,
They are not wrong in this.   I often warned
The youth of Berne, the nobles to avoid
To give offence, by haughty sneer, to those
That are by birth not noble.   Why?   Above
All things, the nobleman must show himself
A *noble man*, magnanimous in deed
And sentiment, in lofty virtues give
Example to the lowly, ignorant;
Be courteous, kind, forbearing to the ones
That earn, by daily toil, their bread, be just
To them, and ever ready to protect,
Defend their rights, uplift the fallen ones,
And bring them back upon their duty's path;
Assist them in their struggles, needs.   Ah, friends:
If we oppress the poor, despise the hand
That works, or soon or late, th' avenging GOD
Will bring us down, perhaps, below themselves,
Beneath their yoke.   My Lords of Berne, beware!
The world is going onward, leveling more
And more the difference of caste, and throws
Aside, like garments torn and old, the whims

And prejudice of former times, and men
Of innate worth alone will rise and stand,
Direct events and issues great, and, though
From lowly source they may have come, they will
By toil arrive to stations, where they shall
Eclipse the nobleman by birth, and lift
Their heads, with majesty, as noblemen
Of nature.

(RUDOLPH *the page appears and beckons to* JULIA, *who goes towards the door, and disappears behind the scene.*)

Julia. (*Outside.*) Holy Virgin! GOD be praised!
My own beloved brother!

(*Enter* EDWARD *with* JULIA *in his arms, followed by* ALOYS.)

Edward. (*Rushes towards his father, and sinks on his knees before him.*)
Father, here

I am!
Adrian. My son!

(*Sinks backward on his chair into a swoon.*)

Julia. (*Throwing her arms around him.*)
Oh! GOD in heaven! he

Is dying.
Von Hallwyl. No! he breathes, though heavily.
It was imprudent, thus to take him by
Surprise. He was excited much before
You came.

Aloys. We did not know that he was ill.

Von Scharnachthal. (*To von Stein and von Erlach.*)
              My Lords, we better go!

Adrian. (*Opening his eyes.*) Am I awake?
Is this my son? Are you my children here?

Julia. Your own, your Edward, Julia, all you love.

Aloys. (*Approaching and seizing his hand.*) And here
    your friend from Unterwalden.

Adrian.   GOD!
Forgive my weakness and ingratitude!
I am unworthy of Thy blessings all.
My children, you, my friends, around me here—

(*He seizes the hand of* JULIA *and that of* ALOYS, *and joins them
before him.*)

Receive, my son, this hand! 'Tis all I have
To give you; she's my richest treasure.

Aloys. (*Sinking on his knees, overpowered by emotion.*)
                     Thanks,
My Lord! I cannot tell, express in words
My gratitude.

Adrian.   May GOD forever bless
You both! I die contented, happy now.

Julia. Oh, father!

Adrian. Children, friends, farewell! My time
Hath come. Farewell to Berne, beloved Berne,
My native land! My friends, hold fast and cling
Forever to the League! ALMIGHTY GOD:

Preserve——in one——an ever—lasting——bond—
My Fatherland!

[Dies.]

(The orchestra plays a Requiem.)

SCENE III.

The forest of Ranft. NICHOLAS OF THE FLUE is kneeling before the Cross. Midnight.

Nicholas.   "Oh Lord, my GOD, vouchsafe
"To take myself away from me, and let
"Me be Thy own entire! Oh, Lord, my GOD:
"In grace bestow on me, whatever may
"Me nearer bring to Thee! O! GOD, my Lord,
"Take all away from me that might withdraw
"My heart from Thee!"

(Enter HENRY IM GRUND, the pastor of Stanz.)

Henry. (*Aside.*)   He is at pray'r. I dare
Not now disturb him, yet delay is loss,
Perhaps, to all the land.

(NICHOLAS arises, and slowly turns towards the hermitage.)

                         Good evening,
Or rather, morning I should say. 'Tis past
Midnight, my pious Brother.
Nicholas.   Who is here,
In night so dark, some wander'r lonely—lost?
Henry. 'Tis I, your friend Im Grund.

Nicholas.   I ought to know
Your voice, my rev'rend Father, well.
 Henry.   I come
In greatest haste to see you.
 Nicholas.   What mishap
Hath taken place?
 Henry. (*With emotion, and tears in his eyes.*)
     Alas! I hardly know,
How to express my anguish, grief, in words.
What Austria and Burgundy in vain
Have tried to do, the Swiss have done themselves.
Their League—it is dissolved!
 Nicholas.   Dissolved? The League
Committed suicide? But when?
 Henry.   To-day.
The Diet, which you have advised yourself
To meet at Stanz, hath held a last, a wild
And stormy session there. The deputies
In rage accused and cursed each other, till,
At last, they left the council hall at night,
Determined to depart to-morrow, thence
No more to meet again. In vain Soleure
And Friburgh did beseech them all, to save
The League, to cease contentions on their claims
To be admitted as Confederates.
They would withdraw. The grudge of old between
The Cantons Schwytz and Zürich burst, alike

A blazing flame, from hidden caves, where hate
And secret rancor still were burning kept,
And unsubdued by years of peace. The men
Of Schwytz, with furious clamor, brought again
The former cause of quarrel up, recalled
St. Jacob's field,[2] whilst Zürich would reply—
Vociferate but " Greifensee!"[3]

    Nicholas.   It was
An awful deed, that bloody butchery
At Greifensee, of civil feuds a fell
Remembrance, aptest to inflame the men
Of Zürich.

    Henry. Thus they parted. Vainly Zug
And Glaris tried to interfere, and bring
To calm the furious elements—and speak
About the glorious past, the victories
By arms united, won. The raging storm
Of passion seemed to have effaced from hearts
And minds, and swept from memory, the deeds
Of. Grauson, Morat, Nancy,[4] where they all
Had fought against the common foe.

                        Oh, friend!
The Fatherland is sinking!   Here I am
Impelled by grief, despair, to beg, beseech
You—come, and help to save the country!   All
What you can do with GOD and men, oh, try
To do——avert the downfall of the land!

Nicholas. Becalm yourself, my rev'rend Father,—
     go,
Return to Stanz, endeavor to retain
The deputies, and tell them, Brother Claus,
Before the Diet, yet does humbly wish
To say a word!
    Henry.   If there is left a hope
To save the land—it is with you.
    Nicholas.   Forgive!
I am a man, a mortal mere, and GOD
Alone can move the hearts, by selfishness
Misled, to yield to charity; but trust
In Him!
    Henry.   I ought to trust; I am a priest
By office bound, to give example to
The flock to whom I preach the Word of GOD.
And yet, how often will discouragement
And melancholy doubt possess my mind,
When thinking of the ways and deeds of men !
How little yet their nature hath been brought
Beneath the gentle rule of love, as taught
By CHRIST! I feel perplexed, and often lost
Within that darksome labyrinth—the soul
Of man. What mystery is there contained!
The flower from the ground comes forth, exhales
Her sweet perfume towards the sky and—fades;
The bird breaks through his shell, and with

So beautiful around him, sings, in notes
Melodious, a hymn of gratitude
To his Creator—dies, and Mother Earth
Will press them both unto her loving heart
And whisper: Well, my children, you have done,
Fulfilled your mission, now return to dust,
From whence you came, and rest forevermore!
But man—Humanity?   What dark and strange
Enigma to the thinking mind her life
Presents—enigma which, in vain have tried
To solve, the sages of the world!

   Nicholas.   My friend,
'Tis solved—there in the CROSS, THE SIGN OF LOVE,
OF UNIVERSAL BROTHERHOOD.   Through years,
By thousands still to come, through mists of doubt,
Of error, superstition, unbelief,
Through seas of blood and purifying fire,   ·
Humanity will have to pass, to reach
At last her destiny in yonder sign—
The CROSS.   She will awake one glorious morn
And hail her Sabbath day of rest in peace
And love.

SCENE IV.

The council hall of the Diet of Stanz, in Unterwalden.   Seats for
the delegates on both sides in the foreground.   An elevated desk,
with an arm-chair behind it, in the centre   A railing separates the
space, occupied by the delegates, from the background, where out-

siders are standing, CASPAR VON HERTENSTEIN, delegate of Lucerne;
JACOB BUGNIET, of Friburgh; HANNS VON STAAL, chancellor of So-
leure; HANNS TSCHUDI, delegate of Glaris, are seen conversing together
in the foreground.

Bugniet. The Diet is to meet again
To-day.   From what I saw, last evening,
It is to end in naught but broil.   We may
As well depart.   There is no more for us
To do or hope, for Friburgh and Soleure.
  Von Staal: Let us await the issue, friends!   you
   know,
At all events, we have not much to lose.
For if the Switzers' League should perish, we,
The cities, can in covenant unite.
  Von Hertenstein. We must, indeed, protect our-
   selves against
This fiery peasant element, that will
Forever take the lead in questions all,
Dictate, with boorish arrogance, to us,
What must be done.   It can no more be borne.
The city of Lucerne hath been the first
To enter, with the Forest Lands, into
A league for mutual defence, but now
Since black ingratitude is all she reaps
From them, since men are found within their midst,
Who highly stood in office once, that will
In secret schemes contrive to spread revolt
Amongst our own dependents, in the land

Of Entlibuch, Lucerne will be the first
To leave the League.[5]

   Tschudi.   I hope, my Lord, you will
With patience wait another day, before
You take this step so fatal to us all.

   (*Enter* PETERMANN VON STEIN, *and* WILLIAM VON DIESSBACH, *delegates of Berne.*)

   Von Diessbach. Good day, my Lords! What now
      we meet again
Convoked by whom—a priest?

   Von Staal.   The world-renowned
Most pious Brother Claus hath sent, last night,
By him the word to us to wait.

   Von Diessbach.   To wait
For what?

   Von Staal. He hath expressed the earnest wish
To speak to us, before we part, perhaps
Forever.

   Von Diessbach. Does he think he can succeed
With them, to reason bring the obstinate,
Uncourteous churls that have insulted us
And all the cities, now for years?

      (*Enter* HANNS WALDMANN, *delegate of Zürich.*)

                   You, too,
Have come? I thought that you had left the town
Last evening, ere the mob of boors incensed,
With threat'ning yells surrounded us, and we

Could hardly cross the street and gain, behind
Our bolted doors, a refuge safe.

Waldmann.   I heard
Of that disgraceful scene, but was myself
Not present; here I did remain until
The priest of Stanz, with whom I had to speak,
Had left me in the dark. But what? We are
Alone, the cities' delegates, and not
A single Forest Lander here? Will they,
Perhaps, refuse to come? Methinks, it is
Of little import now. It is too late.
The abyss hath become too great between
The cities and the Forest Lands, but we
At least, my Lords, of Zürich, Berne, Lucerne,
And Friburgh and Soleure, united may
Remain, forget the feuds of old amongst
Ourselves, the feuds in which we mostly were
Involved by them, who now insult us.

(*Enter* HANNS ZUMBRUNNEN, *delegate of Uri;* DIETRICH INDERHALDEN,
RAETZI, *Landammann of Schwytz;* HENRY ZELGER, *of Unter-
walden;* HANNS ITEN, *of Zug. Among the spectators in the
background are seen* ALOYS, ARNOLD *and* HENRY IM GRUND,
JOHN VON HALLWYL, EDWARD VON BUBENBERG, HANNS IM
HOF, *of Uri,* HAGEN, *of Soleure.*)

                         Here
They come. They look like angry dogs. Let us
Remain as calm, composed as we can be!
11*

(The delegates from the cities bow, with cold and haughty mien, to those of the Forest Lands, who seem to take no notice whatever of their manner, and abruptly turn to the left side of the hall, where they seat themselves, grouping together.)

Inderhalden. You see, what prospect here we have,
    The proud,
The sneering airs, with which we are received
What is the use to come, renew the scenes
Of yesterday?
    Hanns Iten. The hermit hath not yet
Arrived.
    Zumbrunnen. I hope, that when he comes, he will
Reprove them well for haughty arrogance.
'Tis not in hope, that they will yield, we come;
'Tis but to see their own confusion.
    Raetzi.   Here
We are, the founders of the League; we have
Received Lucerne, and Zürich, Berne within
Our midst. Their wealth, prosperity, would have
Been brought to naught ere this. We all have bled
For them, and now what thanks do we receive?
    Inderhalden. Is it a wonder? What can we expect
From Zürich's traffic-ridden people, who,
For gold or profit, readily will sell
Themselves, their souls unto the evil one?
As long as they could find advantage in
The League, as long as there a penny was
To gain; as long as they could use our arms

To help them in their feuds, we then were called
Confederates, beloved, dear.

   Zumbrunnen.   I am
Not much surprised at Zürich's conduct, grudge
And rancor; treach'rous to the League before,
But forty years ago, and whipped into
Allegiance then, she never will forget
Her own humiliation; but that Berne
Ungrateful Berne! should thus degrade herself
And leave her faithful friends, the Forest Lands,
That have assisted her in need, distress,
So often; Berne, whom we have saved, that she
Should thus affront us, and refuse to grant
The shares of spoil we are entitled to—
'Tis past my comprehension.

   Inderhalden.   Fools that we
Have been! The Lords of Berne look with contempt
On us. They think, we have no right to things
That once belonged to princes, nobles like
Themselves. The cities, they intend to keep,
Withhold from us the booty, rather to
Dissolve the League, than to give up the part
We claim.

   Hanns Tschudi. (Coming into the middle of the scene.)
                My Lords and delegates: would it
Not suit your worships, since we are again
Assembled here, to take our wonted seats?
And whilst we wait, at least, let us observe

The Diet's customary forms, for sake
Of self-respect!

Von Hertenstein. What further need of forms?
The spirit is departed, gone!

Waldmann.   The League
Hath proved to be a failure in the end.

Von Stein. And all the common struggles, toil for
    her,
Have been for naught.   Our fathers, we ourselves
Have bled in vain!

Zelger.   And please, my Lords, to tell
Whose fault it is?

Zumbrunnen.   Who first hath set aside
The covenant that once was formed, by all
Of you consented to, and now is spurned,
And violated, spat upon, by you,
The cities?

Inderhalden. Who refused to us, your own
Companions in arms, the lawful share
Of booty taken from the foe, and who
Hath treated us, with arbitrary hands,
As if we were your subjects mere, and not
Your equals?

Von Diessbach.   Equals? you to us!

Inderhalden.   I knew,
The Lord of Berne would show the cloven foot
At last.

Zumbrunnen. Your equals, no! superiors—
To you we are. W've whipped your betters.

Waldmann. Where?
At Greifensee?

Inderhalden. At Greifensee! so let
It be! There traitors and their allies once
Received what they deserved.

Waldmann. (*Grasping the hilt of his sword.*)

Who dares to call
Us traitors here?

Inderhalden. (*Drawing his sword.*)

I dare, you demagogue,
You sneaking dog!

Waldmann. This calls for blood, revenge!

(*Immense sensation amongst the delegates.* VON DIESSBACH, VON
STEIN, ZUMBRUNNEN, *and* ZÉLGER *throw themselves between*
WALDMANN *and* INDERHALDEN, *who, brandishing their swords*
endeavor to meet.

Enters NICHOLAS OF THE FLUE. *All the delegates uncover their*
heads and make way before him. WALDMANN *and* INDER-
HALDEN *put up their swords, and remain standing each at one*
extremity of the scene.)

Nicholas. (*After a long pause, during which he looks*
around with calm but melancholy dignity, scan-
ning the countenance of each delegate.)
And hath it come to this? Must brothers draw
The sword against each other?

(*All the delegates bend their eyes upon the ground.*)

" Good my Lords,
" Confederates, beloved, faithful : here
" I come, an old and feeble man. I have
" Been called from solitude by one who is
" To me an excellent Father, friend, that I
" Might speak to you about the Fatherland.
" I have nor art, nor science. I am a man
" Unlearned. But what I have, I will impart
" To you from GOD, who saved your fathers oft,
" In times when great distress was threatening
" The land, and who, on days of battle, gave
" You victory.
    " Confederates : why have
" You gone to war? Because it could not be
" Avoided. Say, by what have you obtained
" Your victories ? By strength alone of arms
" United. Now you will dissolve your League,
" On spoils' account? Confederates, I pray,
" Allow no such report to go abroad from you!
" I faithfully advise, I earnestly beseech
" You, from the cities, to dissolve the pacts
" Offensive to your old confederates.
' And you, from Forest Lands, I do entreat:
" Remember how Soleure and Friburgh fought
" For you! Receive them in your League!
" Misunderstandings may 'midst brothers oft
" Arise. When these occur, remain to old
" And equitable custom true! Be just

" And booty, in proportion to the men
" Each Canton sent into the field!

                                 " Do not
" Extend too far the hedge that now surrounds
" You!   Shun to interfere with foreign brawls!
" Be neighbors courteous, kind, and peaceable!
" But whosoever should attempt to crush—
" Oppress you, then let him find—men!   And be
" It far from you, that any one should take,
" Accept, in gold, reward for service to
" The Fatherland!   Beware of factions, strifes
" Amongst yourselves!   They would destroy you all.
" CONFEDERATES, OH BROTHERS!   LOVE YE ONE
" ANOTHER!

                 " May ALMIGHTY GOD, in grace,
" Be bountiful to you, as He hath been
" It heretofore!"[26]

(NICHOLAS *stands with eyes and hands uplifted to Heaven.   The dele-
gates look with emotion, first at him, then at each other.   At last,
in one spontaneous burst of feeling, they rush into each other's
arms, with tears in their eyes.*)

*Hanns Waldmann. (Extending his hand to Inderhal-
den.)*   Forgive!

Inderhalden.   Forget!

Nicholas.   And now,

Be brothers as before; be one, be one,
Be one forevermore!

SCENE V.

The forest of Ranft. Bells are ringing in the distance, in all directions. Now and then, the sounds of Alpine horns are heard. The hermitage of NICHOLAS OF THE FLUE is adorned with garlands of evergreens. JULIA and MARY are sitting on the trunk of a tree in the foreground. LILY is occupied in twining a wreath of flowers at the foot of the Cross.

(LILY *sings :*)

Peace in the solitude,
　　Peace dwelleth here;
Breezes are whispering
　　Peace to my ear.
Gentle and beautiful
　　Voices I hear;
Voices of angels sing,
　　Lingering near :
Peace in eternity,
　　Peace dwelleth here!

Julia.　　　　　　　How sweetly sings
The child! How happy there she looks amidst
Her lovely flower sisters!

Mary.　　　　　　　Happy, now,
Indeed, we all should feel. Was ever there
A day more glorious in the land? You hear—
The bells are ringing all, in village, town,

And hamlet, from the vales of Rhaetia to
The distant chains of Jura, and to-night
The fires of joy, from mount to mount, they will
Be seen, throughout the whole of Switzerland.

    Julia. (*Embracing Mary.*) My darling sister, GOD
        be praised! I think
No greater victory the Swiss have won
Than that we celebrate to-day. *Themselves*
They've conquered ; within their hearts, their own
Resentment crushed.

    Mary.   How wonderful! And all
Is due to him, whose quiet, lone retreat
We have adorned, in gratitude ; whose name
From hence the Swiss will ever bless, exalt—

    Julia. —Imprint in characters indelible
Into their children's hearts the name so sweet,
Melodious, of NICH'LAS OF THE FLUE.

    Mary. I feel so happy, too, that one like you,
My Lady—

    Julia.   Lady—why not sister now ?
Your sister ? Are you not my brother's own
Betrothed ?

    Mary. I hardly dare to dream, as yet,
It can be true that he should love and choose
A simple peasant girl.

    Julia.   Why not ? You are
The very one adapted to himself,
To make him happy. Modest, gentle child :

12

Your quiet ways have won his heart.   I know
My brother.   All he needs is one like you,
To tame his reckless mind.   His heart is true!
   Mary. I know it well.
   Julia.   I should be satisfied,
If all could be so easily arranged
In my affections, as in yours.   Although
My most lamented father did express
His wish, that I should have my choice, and on
His dying bed he placed my lover's hand
In mine, and blessed us both, my relatives
And guardians now object; and though they **all**
Respect the manly worth of him I love,
They say he hath no home.   His real name
Is still a mystery.   My noble friend
Von Hallwyl, and myself, have come to ask
The Brother Claus to tell what he alone
Does know about his birth and parentage.
   Mary. I hope you will succeed ;   but none, **as yet,**
Could ever be enlighten'd on this point.
The Brother Claus will give no answer, when
He's questioned on this subject.
   Julia.   Strange it **is**
That one so noble, highly gifted by
The bounteous hand of nature, should **remain**
In ignorance about his origin.

     (*Voices singing in the distance behind the scene:*)

Is there on earth a happier life
Than that of Switzer herdsmen free ?
On sunny Alps, away from strife
Of *cities'* throng, they sing the glee :
When the morning is dawning,
To the mountain they go ;
And the cow-bells are ringing,
And the little lambs springing,
And the merry boys singing :
To the mountain, to the mountain, to the mountain we go !
Diuli-a, iulia, iuli-a-ho !

(*Enter* NICHOLAS OF THE FLUE, HENRY IM GRUND, JOHN VON HALL-
WYL, *and* ARNOLD IM GRUND. LILY *arises and takes the hand of*
NICHOLAS.)

Lily. Good evening, Brother Claus ! You see
what here
I made for you ?
Nicholas. 'Tis beautiful, my child ;
But as you twined this wreath beneath the Cross,
I think 'tis best adapted to adorn
The CROSS.
Von Hallwyl. (*Aside to Julia.*) Be cheerful, friend !
The Brother Claus
Will speak, he says, in proper time, and soon,
On what concerns you most.

(ALOYS, EDWARD, *and a crowd of herdsmen, peasants, men and wo-*
men, appear on the top of the hill, behind the hermitage.)

The crowd. All hail ! all hail !
To Brother Claus, the saviour of the land !

(*The crowd divides and makes way to the delegates of the Diet of
Stanz.   Each of the latter is preceded by a banneret, bearing the
colors of his respective Canton.*

The crowd. All hail to Brother Claus, the saviour of
The League!

(*Music.   Ringing of bells.   Variations on the Alpine horn in the
distance.*)

Waldmann. (*Stepping forward.*)   Most pious Brother
    Nicholas:
We come to thank you faithfully for all
The care, and labor, and fidelity
With which you have brought blessings on us all.
May GOD reward you in eternity!
    Inderhalden.   From civil war you have preserved
    the land;
For GOD hath given grace unto your words.
    Nicholas.   To Him alone belongs the glory, not
To me.   Prostrate yourselves before His throne,
And, with humility, as children meek,
Confide in Him; and Hé will bless you all!
But now, my friends, a duty yet remains
For me to be performed; and since a crowd
Of witnesses is present here, I may
Not choose a better moment.

(*He beckons to* ALOYS *to come forward.   The latter advances, with
an expression of anxious expectation.* JULIA, MARY, LILY, JOHN
VON HALLWYL, HENRY *and* ARNOLD IM GRUND, *and* EDWARD, *form
a semicircle around him.*)

All of you
Who are assembled here, you know this youth.
Thus far he hath been looked upon as one,
By fell misfortune cast into the world,
To be of charity an object mere.
And yet by innate worth he raised himself
To highest fame, amongst his countrymen.
You've seen him here a modest herdsman, like
The humblest of yourselves. You've seen him, then,
On battle-fields, amongst the first of all
The heroes stand; you know that he refused
The honored title knighthood gives. What need
Had he of title—nobleman by birth?

    Arnold. What, nobleman, you say? Is he of noble
      blood?

    Nicholas. Of noble blood? the noblest of the land!
In Switzerland, no nobler name than his
Is found, revered by all.

    Julia.   Oh, speak, explain!

    Nicholas. Forbear in patience! So that all of you
May understand the reasons, why this youth
Himself was kept in ignorance so long
About his birth, I must declare, that I
Was bound, by solemn promise, given to
His father, on his dying bed. The youth
Was then a babe. His birth had cost a life—
His mother's. Once in deepest night, his sire,
The grandson of a hero, known by all

12*

At home and far abroad, had sent for me.
He begged me to accept in charge the child,
To bring him up amongst the herdsmen of
The land, to keep in secret all about
His noble birth, descent; that he might learn
To love, respect the simple customs which
Have here, within these vales, preserved a home
For FREEDOM and EQUALITY. He asked
That he should well be taught in Christian lore,
Religion's essence : love of fellow-men,
And love of country—safest guarantees
Of states and commonwealths to have, within
Their midst, the source that keeps, refreshes life
Amongst a nation's citizens. And when
To manhood grown, the child should have displayed,
By virtuous actions, worthiness to bear
A noble name, that then alone I should
Inform him of his glorious ancestry.

The time hath come. The youth hath well deserved
Of honors all and

        (Looking with a smile on JULIA.)

          happiness in store
For him. This package, sealed, was left unto
My care. His father's will is here contained.
It leaves, bequeathes to him the whole estate,
His ancestors have held for centuries.

Von Hallwyl. But say! what is his name?

Nicholas. (*Taking Aloys by the hand.*) His name?
Come forth,
And all of you may stand aside, for here
Behold, revere the great-grandson of him,
Who fell at Sempach: ARNOLD STRUTHAN, knight
Of WINKELRÏED!

Julia. (*Falling on her knees.*) Of WINKELRIED!

(*Profound sensation amongst the crowd.*)

Nicholas. And now,
Let me repeat to you the words with which
His ancestor took leave of yours', and fell:
"CONFEDERATES! REMEMBER YE MY BLOOD!"

Henry Im Grund. ALMIGHTY GOD, BE PRAISED
FOREVERMORE!

(*The Angelus rings for the evening. All prostrate themselves. Whilst a single voice sings the "*AVE MARIA, GRATIA PLENA *!" in the distance, the glow of a large bonfire illuminates the scene. The curtain slowly descends.*)

END OF ACT V.

NOTES.

ACT I

1. Page 10. "*Gelobt sey Jesus Christus!*"—Answer: "*In Ewigkeit, Amen!*" This form of pious salutation is still in use in Catholic Germany and the Catholic Cantons of Switzerland, where the German language is spoken.

2 and 3. Page 12. In 1298, the Bernese, under the command of Ulric von Erlach, defeated an army of nobles hostile to their commonwealth at Donnerbuehl, near the gates of the city of Berne. In 1330, Rudolph von Erlach, the son of the former, at the head of 5,500 Bernese, and their allies from the Forest Cantons, obtained a victory over an army of nearly 20,000, in the battle of Laupen.

ACT II.

1. Page 44. "*A model State, by wisdom, justice ruled.*" John von Muller, in his history of the Swiss Confederacy, pays the following tribute to the old aristocratic government of Berne:

"In the whole extent of the history of mankind, it will not be easy to find a commonwealth which, for so long a period, was administered with more wisdom and integrity, on the whole, and would have better deserved to last forever, than that of Berne." (Vol. I, page 460, note 117.)

2. Page 53. The reader will recollect that in 1476, all the Swiss Cantons were still Catholic.

ACT III.

1. Page 59. "*Magnifiques Seigneurs de Berne*" was the title by which the members of the aristocratic government of that Canton were addressed.

2. Page 62. See John von Müller's Geschichte der Schweizerischen Eidgenossenschaft, vol. V, page 50.

3. Page 74. "*The Cross of Schwytz*," &c.

4. Page 74. "*The key of Unterwalden*," &c.—A small, white cross, in the right corner of a red field, is seen in the armorial escutcheon of Schwytz, whilst that of Unterwalden has a white key in a red field.

5. Page 75. "*Naefels saw victorious,*
　　　Fridolin, thy sainted patron," &c.
The battle of Naefels, in the Canton of Glaris, was fought on April 9, 1388, two years after that of Sempach. Six thousand Austrians were completely routed by 530 Swiss. St. Fridolin, the patron Saint of the Glarners, appears on their escutcheon.

ACT IV.

1. Page 82. Von Muller's Geschichte, &c., vol. V, page 52.

2. Page 96. Ibid, page 69.

3. Pages 97–8.—Translation :

"From the depths, oh Lord, this day we all come crying unto Thee, King, Creator of all angels and men, hear us praying! Do not despise our voices, holy, everlasting God, Judge of nations! In such great danger, oh Lord, grant unto our people, through the strength of prayers and through Thy grace, victory and lasting peace! May the glory of Thy kingdom and mercy last; may Thy name be holy for all ages to come! Amen!

ACT V.

1. Page 109. " *The felon's doom awaits his last remains, his ashes.*" The bodies of insolvent debtors were doomed to be buried near a place, where dead animals were interred.

2. Page 120. " *St. Jacob's field.*"—This memorable battle was fought near the city of Basil, in 1444, during the wars of the Swiss against the city of Zurich, which had seceded from the League, and was assisted by the Emperor of Germany and the King of France in her struggles against her old confederates. Fifteen hundred Swiss attacked an army of 30,000 Armagnacs, who, headed by the Dauphin, afterwards Louis XI, king of France, had come to the relief of Zürich. The brave band of the Swiss was overpowered and almost entirely annihilated, not, however, until their enemy had 8,000 killed, and lost 1,500 horses.

3. Page 120. " *Greifensee* "—During the civil war, alluded to above, the castle of Greifensee, defended by a detachment of dependents of Zurich, was taken by the Swiss Confederates. Sixty of the garrison were executed in one day, by order of Itel Reding, the commander of the troops of Schwytz.

4. Page 120. It was in the battle near Nancy that Charles the Bold lost his life.   About 8,000 Swiss had come to assist René, Duke of Lorraine, in recovering his realm.

5 Allusion is made here to Peter am Stalden of Entlibuch, who was concerned in a conspiracy against the government of Lucerne. Some of the prominent men of Unterwalden were said to be implicated in the plot, for which Am Stalden was executed.

6. Page 131. See Von Müller's Geschichte, &c., vol. V, page 253. The whole address is taken from the old chronicles.

CPSIA information can be obtained
at www.ICGtesting.com
Printed in the USA
LVOW04s0415030116
468874LV00023B/380/P